Thomas Coffin Amory

Siege of Newport

Thomas Coffin Amory
Siege of Newport
ISBN/EAN: 9783337156510

Printed in Europe, USA, Canada, Australia, Japan

Cover: Foto ©ninafisch / pixelio.de

More available books at **www.hansebooks.com**

SIEGE OF NEWPORT.

BY

THOMAS C. AMORY,

AUTHOR OF "LIFE OF GENERAL JOHN SULLIVAN,"
"GOVERNOR JAMES SULLIVAN," ETC.

———•———

CAMBRIDGE:
JOHN WILSON AND SON.
University Press.
1888.

CONTENTS.

Canto		Page
	Introduction	1
I.	Landing	17
II.	Sea Fight	28
III.	The March	46
IV.	The Siege	58
V.	The Battle	74
VI.	Iroquois	105
VII.	Savannah	112
VIII.	Surrender	146
	Centennial	153

SIEGE OF NEWPORT.

INTRODUCTION.

SHOULD he who reads these unpretending lines
   Inquire why venture on so bold a theme, —
Ours but to follow; Providence designs
We tread the paths, the paths of duty seem.
If circumstance beyond our own control
Guide, shape resistlessly our aims and ends,
But weak the faith, if our poor human soul
Upon its own unaided strength depends.
From early youth my vernal seasons spent
Amidst the enchantments of this lovely land,
To whom the siege a deeper interest lent
From that near kinsman under whose command
In freedom's cause the dauntless patriots fought,
And justly claimed the well contested field:
That victory with consequences fraught
Forced foreign rule our independence yield.

Besides, the wingèd words are now my own
That flew from ship to shore that bloody day;
Till, every doubt to firm conviction grown,
I heard a voice I dared not disobey.
Moreover, conscious often prejudice
Poisons the mind too eager to defame,
Those nobler planned will deem it not amiss
If shown how undeserved reproach or blame;
Or if familiar its historic ground,
The memories with which these scenes aglow
In simple truths so much for feeling found,
In rhythmic measures should the story flow.

That August day, how long remembered well,
With generous Randolph round this winsome isle
We rolled delighted over field and fell
Along its graceful shores for many a mile;
The azure sky in lofty arches bent,
The wide-spread seas with golden lustre smiled;
A summer haze its soft enchantment lent,
As genial converse swift-winged hours beguiled.
Off from Fort Adams pealed the morning gun
As for our quest we rose refreshed and strong,
Yet near its couch still beamed the morning sun,
As tireless dashed our lusty steed along.

The billowy breakers thud upon the beach,
Then up the slopes their swelling waters sweep,
Till crest with foam the splashing fetlocks reach,
And back the pebbles wash in cadenced song.
Their swift pursuers, gathering in the deep,
In order due speed on the hopeless chase,
Join in the yeasty tumult of the shore,
Glide up and mingle with the refluent tide;
Then, vigor spent, their downward steps retrace,
Roll slowly back and in the ocean hide,
Whose healthy pulses beat for evermore.

Beyond the surf the early bathers swim,
Cool off their fevered brows, forget their care,
In vigorous sport throw out the frolic limb,
Dive through the toppling waves, their turmoil share;
And maidens fair and gallant knights dash by,
Their flashing hoofs keep time with even tread
To jocund voice as merrily they fly,
The splashing drops their pearly moisture shed,
As on they speed between the waves and sky.

Steeped in the early beams, the swelling sides
Of Honeyman look down upon the sea,
On many a white-winged craft in silence glides,
Its special mission wrapt in mystery;

On sumptuous palaces that line the cove,
Whose terraced lawns creep down the crumbled
    rock,
Whose gardens trim and many a clustered grove
In kind embrace this bay of beauty lock.

Fording the stream that flows from Laundry brook,
Ploughing the sands enclose this world-known
    beach,
Climbing the heights, from off its crest we look
On summer sheen far as the eye can reach;
The sun-steeped cliffs, the fretted sea between,
Yon ancient mansion in its quiet nook,
The shattered elms that wrap its roof in green,
Its spacious barns whole flocks and herds might
    hold,
The veils of mist their phantom forms enfold,
Entránce whoever gazes on the scene.

Bound by its spell we lingered till our quest
Regained its strength to speed us on our way;
Then down the steep incline to Sachuest,
Scanning the marvels of its spreading bay, —
Where Purgatory's darkened caves proclaim
Woe to the tempted on its slippery brink,
Who, heeding not the sorrow or the shame,

INTRODUCTION.

What is most pleasant, not most wise, prefer;
What briny waters must be theirs to drink
Before regained the regions of the blest!
That Paradise which near gave welcome rest
To Berkeley, the minute philosopher
Who every virtue under heaven possessed.
His life exemplified the faith and love
Which as a bishop of his Church he taught,
Yet who denied to man the power to prove
Matter existing but in human thought.
He helped the course of empire wandering west,
Endowed a college with his fertile lands:
Lo, where his home dilapidated stands.
He often left this Paradise to roam,
And where the hanging rocks approach the sea,
Feasting his sight upon the sparkling foam,
His inward eye, absorbed in revery,
Undazed by light, went ranging bold and free
Through all the mazes of philosophy.

Near where thus Berkeley wove his tangled skein,
Crowds clustered on the beach our course delay;
For, as in Holy Writ, the fisher's seine
Draw finny myriads from their sportive play, —
The mass, menhaden, to enrich the soil,
The few, more precious, to refresh their toil.

Perchance in yonder lichen-mantled barn,
Its hoary sides by blasts from ocean worn,
Some ancient crone still spins her daily yarn,
The muzzled ox still treadeth out the corn,
The fresh-made ricks hid in sequestered nooks,
Await their turn for fickle winds to grind;
These simple souls, though not unversed in books,
In their sires' footsteps their best wisdom find.

Had we no sacred graal for our quest,
What joy with skies like these our paths to leave,
'Mid hedges wild and rustling branches rest,
Happy in Nature that cannot deceive;
Visit these old abodes now gray with age, —
Perhaps were old when Berkeley roved about,
Crossing their thresholds as a priest or sage,
To cure infirmity or settle doubt;
These homes transmitted down from sire to son
May harvest legends of their modest fate,
Of those whose thread of life was deftly spun,
Better worth while than theirs the world calls great.

With quickened pace by Sachuest point we speed,
Where fashion's votaries gathered for the race,
And merry crowds flock there on foot and steed, —
Gentle and simple find a welcome place.

Few scenes more brilliant has the past to tell,
Than when, collected on its ample ground,
The sunny surges round us heave and swell,
Against its rocky battlements resound;
Now from the happy throngs around the lists
The merry voices make the welkin ring,
As the last horse with measured stride persists,
And wins the race with one impassioned spring.
And as the distant hills in queenly grace
Purple beneath the sun's declining beams,
The frolic mass their hurried course retrace,
The crescent moon above the sunset gleams.

Seconnet's beach that opens on its bay,
With dreams of times long vanished, we explore;
Now in the tangled paths pursue our way
To where the learned Angell lives no more.
Long to his dull career no glory came;
He read and pondered o'er his musty books,
Till works more widely treasured gild his name,
Give law to tidal waters and to brooks.
There, afterwards, the gifted Arnold dwelt,
Wrote the proud story of his native State;
Whose noble soul a generous ardor felt
For all the just and true, the wise and great.

Along Seconnet by the Indian road,
Perhaps the same Canonicus pursued,
Which with his royal following he trode
Before the white men on his realms intrude;
By Fogland ferry, Compton, grim and trist,
Crossed to reach the Island of the Mist
By Barstow's hall, embosomed in the trees
Of his own planting, various and rare,
Whom all this lovely Eden failed to please
When winter came and he was lonely there;
By grand Vaucluse with all its mystic lore,
Gardens and groves and lawns that reach the shore.
But we press on, for not for me to tell
Of those created and in bliss possessed.
Yet saddened memory may one moment dwell
Upon that noble pair among the blest,
Whose beauty, culture, taste found here a name,
With all to make an earthly paradise;
Yet all too soon the fatal summons came,
Released her spirit to its kindred skies:
His anguished soul found solace in his faith,
And other ties insured a happier life;
Yet these enchanting grounds still haunt the wraith
Of all was loveliest in the child or wife.
Long since this shrine of checkered memories
Passed on to one whose race, though multiplied

In all its branches, has the power to please;
Esteemed, beloved, without one taint of pride.
'T is said that many a phantom hovers still
About its chambers, yet inspire no dread,
Whose cheerful creed persuades all may that will
Have ghostly converse with the loved and dead.

Still farther on a spacious mansion stands;
Its form and tints suggest provincial days,
When the rich few monopolized these lands
And spent their substance in baronial ways.
For those who best enjoy this fair domain
Flows in their veins blood for a noble pride;
The glorious Emmett, who, without a stain,
To free his country for his country died.

The eastern road leads onward to the gates
To Crundell's mills, best as Glenanna known, —
For her whose youthful loveliness the fates
To all that makes true womanhood has grown.
This tangled glen for generations yields
The choicest pleasure to all Nature love;
Not in its wealth of cultivated fields, —
It forms throughout a consecrated grove.
Beneath its ancient shades an amber stream
Rushes and falls in many a wild cascade;

Its mouldering mill seems but a troubled dream,
Long ages since its busy wheels have played.
But here, where Channing often came to muse,
Fashion delights to wander from its path;
Lovers its coverts for communion choose;
The merry clam-bait often builds its hearth;
Near by, its modest tea-house, simple, plain,
Often attracts the gayest of the gay,
Whose hearts beat music to the loveliest strain,
As blush of morning opens on the day.

Another hour along by Quaker Hill,
Across the vale once red with kindred blood,
We reached the mouldering battlements that still,
As when upon that famous day they stood,
Their graceful walls lift high 'bove field and flood;
For hours soon sped we gazed upon the scene
Not greatly changed, save now Seconnet spanned
By bridge and rail, and now the herbage green,
Where once ten thousand men in battle stand
The sultry noonday, fighting hand to hand,
Till freedom waves her banner to the sky
As her brave sons shout out their victory.
We strolled for long about this battle-field,
And conjured into life the ranks opposed;

Witnessed their onslaught, where compelled to yield,
The British rout, the well-fought battle closed.

Our horse we baited down at Anthony's,
Where Greene, that bloody day, in season sped,
His valiant troopers hid behind the trees
While his brave staff should break their daily bread.
The warning came of Hessians marching near, —
The savory meat abroil upon the fire;
Not caring much which should the first appear,
Not till the steak's consumed would he retire.
We saw the marks of bullets on the wall;
The aged grandchild of the owner then
Told us how in the fight the cannon ball
Hissed o'er the roof, and fell in neighboring glen;
For many a year still traced the marks of strife
Where that hot day strong, fierce, and fearless men
In desperate combat struggled, life for life.

Our steed refreshed, with rapid steps conveyed
To Bristol Ferry two most famished souls;
With pleasant dames our late repast we made
Till all forgot fatigue from morning strolls.

Four hours since noon; not many more were left
For what remained to see or do that day;
Oft from the bay the freshening breezes swept
As by its shore we took our homeward way.
Down by the iron mines we hold our course,
Along their steep decline our weary feet
Explored their depths, — a plentiful resource
Of wealth to Crocker all were glad to greet;
By Portsmouth groves, where in our civil strife
Our wounded soldiers, by the thousand, found
The heavenly care of mother, maid, and wife,
That to the ranks restored them strong and sound.
Not all: in fight were many maimed for life,
The haggard groups limped languid 'bout the
    ground,
For scores of men had lost an arm or leg,
Some writhed with anguish from an angry wound
Till gentle hand applied the soothing salve;
All felt their country would not let them starve,
Or, though disabled, would their children beg.

Then by the glade where gentle genius dwells,
A gifted woman, whose impulsive soul
For every human need instinctive swells,
Her work inscribed on glory's noblest roll.
How well remembered, that romantic glade,

That once was hers, and bears an honored name
Of loveliest maiden in the distant days,
For whom historic men preferred their claim,
Whose beauty still evokes historic praise.
But Polly Lawton's lay in pale eclipse,
While gushed the song or speech from Julia's lips.
In Lawton's valley that bright summer day
A group of men and maids, assembled there,
Strolled through its paths that looked upon the bay,
Or 'neath the shading trees the banquet share.
Surely no lovelier banquet hall than that:
Through the midst flowing fast a copious brook,
The emerald banks on which we lolled or sat
Formed with its lofty ledge a sylvan nook,
Surrounded by a multitude of trees;
And as we lay enchanted in the grass,
Their branches rustling in the cooling breeze,
Our only fear such happy hours must pass, —
She came, and, seated on a log lay there,
Sang to the throng bewitching melodies.

All round about upon the hill-tops strown
Mementos of the times that tried men's souls.
Lo! near the bay, that bastion overgrown
With turf and wild-flowers on its sunny knolls,

Unwasted by the many seasons flown,
Where brave Laurens — upon the battle rolls
None honored more — that morning stood his ground
Until the Hessians his small force surround.
Malsbury, their guide, tells how on gallant steed
He, garbed in green and white, his ranks deployed
(Part Continentals in their white and blue),
Kept long these purchased aliens employed,
And when out-numbered, undismayed withdrew.
Both sides fought bravely, both as freely bled.
The Southern knight his orders then obeys
To save his troops unharmed for future stead,
Falls fighting back, where wall or thicket lays;
Watching his chance, pours in his volleyed shot,
And when the foe came up they found him not.

In yonder mansion, Barton with his band
Pounced down upon the Governor surprised;
With muffled oars they on the bay-shore land,
And though a hostile army near at hand,
On such a quest all thought of risk despised.
Prescott, who then exchanged for Sullivan
Taken with Sterling in Long Island's fight,
Now ranking second in the garrison,
Commanded here perhaps upon the right;

His chief, Sir Robert, distant in the town,
On him devolved the battle for the Crown.
In seventy-five, when our own Prescott led
His troops to Charlestown for that earlier strife,
More than a thousand of their foemen bled,
Crippled in battle, or deprived of life.
In seventy-eight, in the engagement here,
The British losses from the morn to night,
From sources quite unquestionable, appear
Equal to that on Bunker's famous height.

By Anderson's and Redwood speeding on,
And where the mother of Greene's grandsons dwells,
Along the cove once owned by Coddington,
Whose pebbly beach the coming storms foretells,
As gorgeous sunset flames, then slowly fades,
We scale the slopes of Tammany which stand
A natural fortress that no art parades,
To shield its rooted walls by sea or land.
This the whole garrison, should disaster come,
Were to have held till succor reached the shore;
But few had seen again their distant home
Had D'Estaing waited but a few days more.
Its heavy guns commanding the approach
To Newport, where a fleet could do it hurt,

The Admiral, if heedless of reproach,
Still shrank from perils he might not avert.

The twinkling stars were bursting through the blue,
Our tireless steed observed his stable near,
And my good friend, as noble and as true
As that Virginia stock he claimed his own,
Refreshed our weary frames with ample cheer,
Well earned by toils that we but little knew,
So pleasantly the busy hours had flown.
Though the swift decades as a vapor fled,
And nearly two since our farewell was said,
I hope his eye may scan this grateful line
With treasured memories as fond as mine.

CANTO I.

LANDING.

For many years our patriot sires
    Had battled with the foe,
At Concord and at Bunker Hill,
    Exchanging blow for blow.
Their cannon planted on the heights
    Had driven him from the town
Where Liberty was cradled,
    And had to manhood grown.
At Brooklyn, against thrice their odds
    They fought the morning through;
Before a second morning dawned,
    Their ranks, unharmed, withdrew.
That autumn, though out-numbered,
    The foe was held at bay,
Till, foiled, he yielded up the field,
    From Chester marched away.
At Christmas, down the Delaware,
    Seeking the Hessian fold,
Captive were led a thousand men,
    Purchased with British gold.

The banks of Brandywine were drenched
  With streams of British blood,
And when the summer sun went down
  They still unconquered stood.
At Bemis Heights and Bennington
  Deserted all the farms;
The enemy's six thousand men
  To Gates laid down their arms.
A few short weeks of rest had sped;
  Re-marshalled their array,
They fell upon the slumbering camps
  Which all unconscious lay.
Chances of war untoward,
  Mistake and fog and smoke,
Snatched victory from their very grasp
  As ranks in panic broke.
Once more that year opposing hosts
  Confront with purpose dread,
But Howe declined the combat
  And home his forces led;
He had in Philadelphia found
  Delights he loved too well,
And quite content to keep his ground,
  Cared not to break the spell.
Another campaign sure to crush
  What left of rebel power;

Yet midst the whirl of pleasure's rush
    Dull thoughts would claim their hour.

At Valley Forge, that winter long,
    Our sturdy veterans bore
Hunger and cold unmurmuringly,
    Disease that tried them sore.
Those gloomy months, forlorn and dread,
    What chance for half-starved men?
When hoped alliance made with France
    Strengthened their hearts again.
Anxious but not disheartened,
    Still stanch for liberty,
Good news came speeding from the North,
    Good news across the sea.
Success brings over hosts of friends,
    Fellow-feelings make one kind
And grateful to whom succor sends,
    To selfish motive blind.
For now upon the ocean wave
    Came flocking near a score
Of vessels vast with soldiers brave;
    Saint Louis' flag they bore.
Howe knew his danger, and aware
    The French would burn his fleet
If left within the Delaware,

Prepared for his retreat.
It was no pleasant thought to leave
   A place so much endeared;
Yet winds and waves his fears deceive,
   Or else the fate he feared.
For eighty days storms blocked the path
   Of ships that sailed the sea;
Britons in season fled from wrath,
   Lest tarrying fatal be.
Of royal stock, if tale be true,
   Commanding for the Crown,
Howe had denied assistance due
   To Burgoyne, marching down;
Clinton, the second in command,
   Appointed to his place,
More fit for what the times demand.
   The allied troops to face,
To intercept, down from the hill
   Our army swept its course,
And war had ended, but self-will
   Had paralyzed Lee's force.

As in the desert fevered lips
   Yearn for the cold and rain,
Keen eyes that sought the promised ships
   Watched long for them, in vain.

At last, where sky and ocean meet,
   A crowd of sails in view, —
Their gladdened eyes with welcome greet
   The French, as near they drew.
Huge monsters of the deep, inside
   Twelve thousand battle-bred
Sailors and soldiers, as they glide
   To port, all canvas spread.
The waving banner, pealing gun,
   Announce the tidings 'long the coast;
Despatches sent by Washington
   Speed on from post to post.
The chiefs in council to direct
   The force with best success;
As shoals and straits New York protect,
   Strong forts prevent access,
To Providence were orders sent
   For preparations fit,
And Sullivan every effort lent
   For what the times permit.
For near two years, Saint George's flag
   On Newport's ramparts flaunts,
And now the hope the place may fall
   Before the fleets of France.
His army's but a scanty force
   For sixty miles of bay,

Should hostile troops from Newport cross
    To pillage, burn, or slay.
But Pigott wasted not his strength
    Reserved for stress of war,
And when the fleet arrived at length,
    Was stronger than before,
Behind his double lines of forts,
    Flooded lagoons and bastions,
With cannon bristling from the ports
    From Easton's cove to Coddington's.
Six thousand well-armed troops defend
    Fair Newport of the sea-girt isle, —
Hessians whom sordid princes lend,
    Britons who freeborn rights defile,
To help enslave their kinsmen here,
    Who fighting for the rights of men
Might rather look for words of cheer
    Than brutal deeds to shame the pen.
Near by some dozen ships afloat,
    Or sunk the channel's course to bar,
Battalions on Conanicut,
    As many on Butts Hill afar,
To guard the fertile farms that spread
    With ripening grain from shore to shore,
To Brenton's point, Seconnet's head,
    A dozen sunny miles or more.

The year before, nine thousand men
   Strove hard to take the place;
But all their efforts spent in vain,
   Spencer his steps retraced.
Not easy, from a land so bare,
   Its stock used up, unripe its grain,
From off its farms a man to spare,
   Or should they come, sustain;
To raise his force ten thousand strong,
   For twice as many furnish food,
Whatever might the siege prolong,
   Provide for all that multitude,
Ovens and flour for the French,
   Tents, guns and powder, flocks and herds,
From grudging men what left them wrench,
   Resentment calm with kindly word.
Unwonted haste is apt to fret,
   War, cruel in its gentlest guise,
In such temptation, how forget,
   To children's lips their bread denies.

Sullivan left no task half done;
   His force two thousand told;
As many sent by Washington
   Had proved at Monmouth bold.

Far more were needed, since as yet
    No foothold gained upon the isle;
No feebler force could foothold gain,
    Guarded by pickets mile by mile.
When Boston once beleaguered lay
    By rebels from the region round,
Enlistment up, they would not stay,
    Leaving their camp unguarded ground;
The waters frozen, and their line
    From Mystic mouth to Savin Hill,
Our armies could less well combine,
    While British troops worked now with will.
He sent forthwith a messenger
    To Weare, for his immediate aid;
Nor long before the succors came,
    Stalwart and hardy, bold yet staid.
And now with like appeal again
    He fired each heart and nerved each hand;
Ere filled the moon, ten thousand men
    Stood armed, equipped, at his command;
Enough expert to drill the rest,
    Among them veterans in fight.
The patriot's ardor warmed each breast
    To battle for their common right;
From bench and bar, workshop and plough,
    Physicians came, priests left their flocks,

The marts of trade in silence now,
    As brave men seized their firelocks
From youth their safeguard, joy, support,
    That rarely missed their steady aim;
To ply the bayonet, scale the fort,
    They heard the call, and instant came.
What they most cherished, risked in war,
    Their toilsome lives left less to learn;
Plain oft might be the garb they wore,
    Beneath, their hearts with fervor burn.

Meanwhile the gallant admiral,
    With all his ships in brave array,
Swept round Point Judith's troubled wave
    And anchored in the bay.
The open roadstead his to keep
    Until his allies close at hand.
Fearing some hostile fleet might sweep
    With favoring breezes to the land,
Perhaps with succors to the town,
    At disadvantage take becalmed,
Or garrison, despondent grown,
    Content with safety, flee unharmed, —
Not strange that he impatient grows,
    Since Byron sails the sea;

Newport defiant, well he knows
    His ships in jeopardy.
The British craft that ply the bay
    Are burnt, and at Seconnet's cape
Three sturdy frigates block the way
    To reinforcement or escape.
A garrison at Butts's Hill
    The passage from its heights command;
Should rebel force at Crundell's mill
    And French near Dyer's island land,
They may be captured; or, if dare
    Dispute the crossing, boats assail,
The frigates sweep the region bare, —
    Such weak resistance not avail.
But as our troops reach Tiverton,
    The British regiments withdrawn
Left Butts's Hill unoccupied;
    Which when the sun at dawn betrayed,
    The patriots, speedily arrayed,
Crossed to the island side.

D'Estaing knew they were coming, and each ship
    Forcing its way moved up towards the town,
Clearing for action, and its anchors trip,
    Prepared for battle as the sun went down.

The following morning as it left the sea,
    The Americans on to the island crossed;
No force opposing and the passage free,
    No idle moment in that crossing lost.
At early daybreak Lafayette, despatched,
    Informed D'Estaing that they his orders wait;
Urge him to land upon Conanicut
    The troops of France, from thence to pass the strait
To join their allies, as proceeding down
    They come abreast where he designed to land;
And, thus united landward of the town,
    Present a force were idle to withstand.
The French contingent, and a thousand more
    That had been left by Sullivan on the main,
Should as concerted several days before
    Under command of Lafayette remain.

CANTO II.

SEA FIGHT.

NEWPORT, an ancient city,
    Still of no less renown,
Streets clustered close together,
    From the hill-top sloping down,
Crowded with handsome structures,
    Many bordering on the bay,
Where with their guns all loaded
    The French fleet ready lay.
Its commerce had been prospered;
    Homes of elegance and wealth
Adorned their pleasant parlors
With all was rich and rare,
With the glory of maidens wondrous fair,
Famed the world over beyond compare,
    Not alone for beauty,
    But for grace and health.

Ten thousand souls possessed it,
    Six thousand soulless men;
One common grief depressed it, —
    So fair, to perish then.

Perhaps some prayer ascended
    From hearts forlorn below;
    Supplications blended
It might be spared the blow.
    It was a scene of horror,
    Of horror and dismay;
Well might strong hearts be breaking,
    And proudest spirits pray.
They felt the hour must surely come
    To sweep them out of life,
    Destroying their lifelong home
    Exposed to deadly strife.

Pigott, the stern commander,
    Burned all his ships of war,
And dwellings caught like tinder
    As winds the embers bore;
Their crackling boards and rafters blaze,
    With maddening fury roar,
Dark wreaths of smoke wrap roof and spire, —
    It seemed that all must go;
And as the conflagration spread
    Midst tribulations dire,
The stoutest men grow still with dread,
Weak women with their terror craze,
And tears of anguish flow.

We know from one who tells the tale,
    And she was there to see,
The piteous moans, the hearts that fail
    In such extremity;
How mother, frantic, grasps her child
    With hopeless woe and wail,
The gentle maids of manners mild
With senseless terror dazed and wild,
    Strong men with terror pale.
Down in the cellars, anxious groups
    Cling madly in despair,
Awaiting there their common doom
Shrouded in universal gloom,
    Which even some among the troops
    Of sturdy veterans share.
It was an awful thought, to think
    Of their impending fate;
Yet their commander would not shrink
    From what his rules dictate,
Though a whole city on the brink
    Of such destruction wait.

Sir Robert, steadfast, stubborn, stood
    Amidst his suppliants pale;
Surrender shames his hardihood
    Whatever power assail,
    A soldier's duty not to quail,

But rather die on battle-field
Than or to man or woman yield.
   And should the enemy prevail,
Would not be shed their blood:
     Perhaps he still has faith in chance,
     Perhaps in heavenly care,
     Perhaps, as knighthood in his lance,
In his armed soldiers there.

D'Estaing was haughty, stern, and proud,
   Often jealous and unjust;
But his worst foes his worth allowed
   When he returned to dust.
His heart was tender, honor keen
   Prompted each word and deed;
And gazing on the lovely scene,
   What marvel that his heart should bleed
   To desolate the place!

Such misery the sternest breasts might melt,
   His own too loving not that misery share;
Perhaps a fervent suppliant he knelt,
   Invoking God that hapless people spare.
Our supplications ever reach His throne,
   Are often granted by His will divine;

If not, we leave events to Him alone,
    And never at His providence repine.
Not always in the mode we blindly pray
    His love and mercy to our needs dispense;
The boon is granted in some other way
    Than seems the fittest to our feebler sense.

If, like the snowy peaks that pierce the sky,
    D'Estaing was of a temper cold and proud,
His heart for others beat with sympathy,
    Indifferent only to the selfish crowd.
No danger daunted him, no sleepless night
    Impairs the vigor of that strong, stern man
Who never swerved from what he deemed the right;
    When once decided, rarely changed his plan.
His captains gave their views at his request;
    He heard in silence what they each might say,
And then deciding what to him seemed best,
    Naught left for them but what he bade, obey.
All through the fleet his arbitrary power
    Enforced with rigor what his needs demand;
If spirit haughty and his temper sour,
    Not less for that well fitted to command.
His favorites few, not all for worth preferred, —
    Such the reproach that often envy made

Which deemed on others benefit conferred
  Implied for self some lack of courtesy.
Some feared and hated, yet esteemed him too
  As an accomplished seaman, wise and brave;
How oft in anguish passed his nights they knew,
  And yet no sign of what he suffered gave.
With thoughtful steps he paced his quarter-deck,
  There and in his cabin lived alone, —
If loved or not, he was too proud to reck.
  Yet naught concerned his fleet to him unknown;
His soul for glory yearned, yet laurels sought
  Were less his own than for the brow of France;
Nor cared if dripping with his heart's blood bought,
  Could they her grandeur or her fame enhance.
Though pain and pride his nobler traits obscured,
  His natural instincts were of knighthood's best;
  His disappointments patiently endured,
  When duty called, he gave himself no rest.
Savannah, Saint Lucie, and Newport now,
  With fault or failure blurred a proud career;
Granada's fillets justly graced the brow
  He laid upon the block without a fear.

No sunshine could dispel that heavy gloom
  That brooded darkling o'er this fated town,
When thirty sail around Point Judith loom,

Rise into view, then drop their anchors down.
These startling tidings sped from Beavertail,
    Confirmed aloft upon the " Languedoc,"
Not unadorned came to the Admiral
    From watch on hill and cliff, from crag and rock.
Too wise to doubt that well this numerous fleet
    Might bring the needed succor to the place,
If Byron with them cut off his retreat,
    He chose to meet the danger face to face.
He issued orders to his troops on land
    Without delay forthwith to re-embark;
Impatience helped not, with few boats at hand,
    Nor all aboard before the night grew dark.
How weak the force opposed to him unknown,
    Or how disheartened were the garrison,
Or Newport would that night have been his own,
    The work he came to do, been bravely done.

When broke the morn, his preparations made,
    Fresh breezes blowing from the west and north,
As ebbs the tide he braves the cannonade
    From Dumpling's and a work that opposite
Stood, where Fort Adams frowns her thousand guns;
    And losing four-score men, he issued forth
To find the enemy the battle shuns.
    Discerns far off Howe with his numerous fleet

Hull down against the sky in full retreat.
He could not tell but that his crafty foe
  Had sailed away the better to contend,
He would have stayed and laid the city low,
  With such assistance as the troops might lend.
If for return, the breezes barred the gate,
  The summer winds were apt to veer and change;
A few short hours might not have proved too late
  To bring the town again within his range.

Lost in conjecture as to what might mean
  That sudden coming, why they now withdrew,
He did not hesitate, lest though still seen
  The enemy might disappear from view.
As the last vessels from the straits defiling
  Float on that August sea without a cloud,
Its sapphire floor with golden dimples smiling,
  As waves on waves in fretted silver crowd;
From off the lofty decks the wide horizon
  Spreading away into the vast expanse,
All tremulous with luminous commotion,
Swelling and heaving from the depths of ocean,
  The keels of nearly twenty ships of France.

No moment wasted; each ship took its place
  In line, as signalled from the "Languedoc;"

Crowding all sail, they followed up the chase
    That flew before them an affrighted flock;
With weather gage, D'Estaing was well content
    To keep his fleet between them and the bay,
Assured that thus his ships could circumvent
    Any attempt to baffle him by day.

Their transports filled with soldiers and supplies
    Clogging their eager efforts to escape,
They know their surest chance of safety lies
    In gaining speedily Long Island's cape;
And as along at night they skirt its shore,
    Their sluggish convoy left where haven found,
Impeded in their onward course no more
    The stancher cruisers o'er the billows bound.
Never asleep when peril hovers near,
    D'Estaing his vigils keeps when others rest;
Nor storm nor battle shook his breast with fear,
    Ever afloat in full equipments dressed.
Not for himself but for his fleet he cared,
For what might chance his tranquil mind prepared;
His only dread, in watches of the night
The foemen would elude his Argus eyes,
For friendly stars emit but little light
    To help the hunter to his feebler prize.

The skies that dawn as clear, the wind as strong,
   As favorable as on the yester morn,
With sails all set, as dashed the fleets along, —
   On the same breeze the hind and panther borne.
They minded not though every sheet was taut,
The yards to their last pressure braced and strained,
Each flaw of wind in some fresh canvas caught,
   As one or other on the distance gained.
They sped along, and now they quit the Sound,
   Double the cape, the crafty hind aware
Byron may come, or other succor found,
   If still pursued within that thoroughfare
   That leads them back to safety and to home.
   Perchance the French might soon give up the chase,
Within fresh perils hardly care to come;
   Perhaps to Newport back their course retrace, —
If not already Newport been relieved
   Through gates his absence had left ajar,
While the Americans march on deceived,
   To be defeated if they press too far.
In vain they reason, D'Estaing falters not;
   Each hour he gains, the distance less and less;
In eagerness to win, Newport forgot,
   He presses sail with utter recklessness.

The azure skies the fleecy cloudlets speck,
Their phantom forms, of many a semblance strange,
Shoot up in peaks or pinnacles, or take
The grand proportions of some mountain range;
Their shadows flitting wildly o'er the seas
 Leave here expanse of brilliancy intense;
Here broader waters deepen into shade,
The air grows sultry and abates the breeze,
The angry surges sweep the vast immense,
 And as the day declines, the sunbeams fade,
The sea all sable and the skies all gloom
 Seemed the sad presage of approaching doom.

While gathered thus the storm, the British fleet,
 Resolved to meet the fate it cannot fly,
Feeling how useless farther to retreat,
 Nor always to the strong the victory.
Some shifting wind that shaped their bold array
 Brought the opposing squadrons side by side,
And port to port their deadly batteries play,
 To mortal combat each their foe defied.
The muttering thunder echoes back the guns,
The raging tempests mingle in the strife;
In battle, death no manly spirit shuns,
But for his country gladly yields his life.

Both fearless fought, and both as freely shed
Their blood for flag, for country, and their cause;
From stem to stern one noble spirit spread, —
To do their duty, not to gain applause.

Amidst the crash of heaven's artillery,
The roar of cannon, and the boisterous gale
Sweeping huge surges o'er the angry sea,
No time nor chance to reef the crowded sail;
And while the quivering timbers reel and rock
Of the great Admiral, the "Languedoc,"
Down came its mainmast with terrific shock.
Such her sad fate predicted from the start;
Her lofty spars soared upward to the clouds,
Successive tempests wrenched her fasts apart,
Her sails were heavy and relaxed her shrouds.
Close by a sister ship, if not as vast,
The "Tonnaut," even more unfortunate;
Its canvas torn and tattered by the blast
Could be to little useful purpose set,
She the same moment lost her mast and sprit,
And floated helpless on the hungry sea.
The sailors sprang to clear away the deck,
To cut apart the ropes, the helm refit,
When two stanch frigates of the enemy,
"Renown" and "Preston," bore down on the wreck.

Crippled by this mischance, the Admiral,
Such bold presumption ill disposed to brook,
　With steadfast mind no peril could appal,
Measures to destroy them with discretion took;
As they wared round to gain a better range
His well-directed broadsides raked and swept,
　Piercing their hulls, their discipline derange,
Their rigging severed and their masts unstept.
　No odds the mariners of England daunt;
The " Preston " strove the " Languedoc " to board,
　Whose batteries above, below, aslant,
Such streams of shot on her assailant poured
That all unmanageable it drifts away
Into the darkness of approaching night,
　Still more obscure from the impending smoke.
Nor could D'Estaing himself renew the fight;
　For midst the mountain waves he helmless lay,
As gale on gale in fiercer fury broke.
One chance he had to sink her, but forbore;
'T is said he had some reason to believe
His combatant was Dutch; perhaps she bore
　The flag of Holland purposed to deceive.

The men on the " Renown " still undismayed,
　Though many slain, and weakened mast and yard,

Closed with the "Marseillais," and long essayed
    To scale her decks, and often pressed her hard.
The French, impetuous, gathered all their strength,
    Repelled their boarders, and their batteries plied
With such effect, their foes content at length
    By waves resistless driven from their side.
Till late that night were heard the booming guns
    Borne on the howling storm from where they fight;
At last each blood-drenched ship the combat shuns,
    Both anxiously await the coming light.

The "Cæsar" in confusion of the night
    Wandered away, and no one whither knew;
Driven by angry tempests in their might,
    Or following up its quarry in its flight,
It dashed along and disappeared from view.
As ceased the storm, and sunshine once again
    Spread o'er the summer sea its azure calm,
Meeting the "Iris" it disabled her;
    Efforts to take her captive proved in vain,
Her consorts near prevented farther harm,
    And leaking sides the boarders bold deter.
It was a bloody battle; port to port
Both bravely fought, nor cared that death was near.
When over, each a friendly haven sought;
The "Cæsar" found a cordial welcome here.

The captain in the onslaught lost an arm;
    His gallant conduct won deserved applause;
His timely words resentment helped to calm:
    He would have given both for such a cause.

Shattered, forlorn, now moored on George's Bank
    That fleet of France, but late so strong and proud.
Bitter the cup their humbled leader drank,
Bitter the thoughts that on his conscience crowd;
His secret pledge on leaving, to return,
Stood out in bold relief, nor could he find,
As various justifications came in turn,
One that could set at rest his tortured mind.
His ships committed to his special care,
Three of six frigates left, in haste to sail,
In the east channel perhaps poorly fare,—
How could he to such obligations fail?
And yet should Byron with his ships be there,
The siege resumed could but destruction bring,
Not only would his fleet but others share.
Anticipated ills his heart-strings wring.
At last his spirit, resolute in right,
Bravely concluded to redeem his word;
With all his vessels that were fit to fight,
Nor, now the winds allow, his course deferred.

How large the fleet opposed he could not tell,
Or whither gone; the "Valiant" captured four,
The "Hector," "Thunder," and the "Senegal,"
Burning the "Bombard," but removed before
Its guns and mortars. Had the Admiral,
With the "Fantasque" and "Sagittaire"
As counselled, changed his course to overhaul
Three ships to windward, he had taken there
Byron, perchance, on board of one of them, —
Byron, his danger and his constant thought,
Who thwarted all his plans by stratagem,
Whom he soon after at Granada fought,
With equal forces upon either side,
And gained by seamanship the victory, —
Some partial solace to his wounded pride
When later he should less successful be.
Eager to learn with whom he had to cope
He followed Howe near by to Sandy Hook,
Whose quickened sail encouraging the hope
His force less than his own, his way he took
To his intended haven; when they reach
The place abruptly left ten days before,
Both Greene and Lafayette in vain beseech,
To take the town, his help for two days more.

Reluctantly he told them the orders of the king,
Should disaster o'ertake him, to Boston to repair.

The hope his fleet returning to drooping spirits bring
Rankled to resentment, vexation, and despair.
Sent to change his purpose an eloquent appeal;
His resolution taken, arguments proved vain,
With temper somewhat ruffled he could scarce conceal,
With his three frigates he sailed away again.
'Tween Nantucket and its shallows
A tortuous course they steer,
Passes that such war-ships never sailed before;
They reached the haven, Byron following near
With all his squadron that had reached the shore.
For many weeks blockaded by his watchful foe,
D'Estaing gnawed his heart in silence and profound regret
That when at advantage he had not struck the blow,
The odds against him had not bravely met.

If in self-excuse he parleyed with irrevocable facts,
Imputing blame where no reproach deserved,
His soul — a soul of honor — readily retracts,
Between the nations friendly ties preserved.
All their means exhausted in protracted war,
What little left them ventured in this throw,
America with reason felt disappointment sore,

In word and action their resentment show.
Hancock and Boston's magnates
Patrol at night the streets
Where sailors and the ruder sort
Infest its low retreats;
Where stinging words, provoking blows,
Led oft to deadly strife,
Which interposing to repress,
Saint Sauveur lost his life.

CANTO III.

THE MARCH.

As thus o'er troubled waters flits the fleet,
  What chanced the army on the sea-girt isle?
Who left deserted, thought not of retreat,
The hoped return their anxious thoughts beguile.
They numbered there ten thousand stalwart men;
The land demands that Newport should be freed, —
Let those that will, march to their homes again,
The greatest glory left for doughty deed.
These valiant troops as gallant chiefs command, —
Greene, Cornell, Varnum, on their native soil;
Hancock, who for the cause pledged life and land,
And Lafayette, whose veins historic boil;
Whipple from Portsmouth, the New Hampshire
      force,
Tyler, Connecticut's contingent led;
Revere from Boston on his tireless horse,
Shepherd and West and Morris, battle bred;
Laurens, whose sire in Congress then presides,
And Livingston, who many a charge shall lead;

Glover, Jackson, Lovell, and a host besides,
Willingly martyrs if the country need.
Nor was their chief less honored than the rest;
Since the war opened, ever in the field,
At times defeated, still he did his best, —
Courage and skill to stronger ranks must yield.
Not one more quick to brave a despot king,
With pen or lip more eloquent or bold;
None to the cause hearts more devoted bring,
Not one more steadfast to that cause uphold.
All knew full well what obstacles beset,
What bloody paths must lead to what they crave,
Nor in presumption ever vain forget
Not theirs to choose the glory or the grave;
And wise to see, when every effort strained
To reach what seems already in their grasp,
When most assured the yearned for prize attained,
Men oft deluded fading phantoms clasp.

Nor over sanguine, without troops and fleet,
Anvil and sledge, small chance to batter down
The double lines which the defence complete,
Reduce the forts encircling the town.
The harbor clogged with sunken ships and wrecks,
Rose Island stretching all along the front
But narrow channels from the sea protects.

Woe to the wooden ships that brave the brunt
Of Tammany and all the batteries fierce
That crowd the heights and guard the graceful shore,
To sweep their decks, their lofty bulwarks pierce!
Yet should D'Estaing victorious return,
The troops in strength already done their part,
Their foes outnumbered would not Newport burn,
Contented if permitted to depart.
Had all his fleet rode safely through the gale,
Howe's found the refuge it was forced to seek,
The Admiral could not in honor fail
To lend his might against a place so weak.
The troops, of all the strength the needs required
To effect the purpose that had brought them there,
Should they give up the advantage and retire,
Well merited the shame were theirs to bear.

They did not rest. To organize their force
Thus quickly gathered, caused some slight delay;
At last prepared to follow up their course,
The march was ordered for the coming day.
The skies had clouded, and the skies had cleared,
At times the thunder pealed, the lightning flashed,
'Mid sudden gusts the August sun appeared,
The rain in torrents on the herbage plashed,
The trickling drops upon each blade and leaf

Returning sunbeams light with golden tint,
And as the distant ships their canvas reef,
The brazen cannon from their port-holes glint,
Ready for battle or to face the storm;
The troops deserted on the hills arrayed
Column or line, order close or open form,
March, countermarch, and wheel and turn and halt,
Then their long ranks stand still for grand parade;
The sun declining down its azure vault
From every sword and moving bayonet glares,
The banners wave, and steeds go prancing by,
And twixt that lovely land and cloudless sky
The bands of France pour forth their martial airs.
In proud array and every man in post,
The general orders, with their clarion sound,
With patriot ardor animate the host,
Responsive cheers reverberate around.

In after orders Sullivan once more
Thanked his brave soldiers, officers and men,
And all who had freely volunteered their aid
To drive the British tyrants from the land;
Their zeal and spirit pleasing presage gave,
The triumph that they sought was near at hand.
In numbers stronger than the enemy,
With sacred love of liberty aglow,

And earnest wish to set the country free;
Fired with resentment at a barbarous foe,
Wherever suffered at his will to go,
Throughout the country desolation spread,
Deluged with blood that unprovoked they shed;
With this to animate and on to press,
The prospect full of promise of success,
Well may they hope a glorious victory.

In bravery tried on many a field of late
Of Continentals long inured to war,
Dependence by their fellow soldiers placed,
Their country, on the character they bore,
Should be another spur to stimulate,
To keep the laurels they had justly won;
The volunteers and independent corps
Of free will came to share the enterprise,
Had every motive to maintain
A reputation which they well might prize,
In promptly flying to their country's call;
State troops had been his privilege to lead,
With everything to lose and much to gain,
He knew none would outdo in gallant deed.

Composed of freemen who the last year fought
With equal courage if not like result,
The same incentives spurred to conquer then

Would give the land like reason to exult.
The expectations by their prowess wrought,
The general safety, property, and life,
Duty as citizens, their rights as men, —
All they most cherished ventured in the strife
Bids act the freeman's part, their birthright claim,
And of Americans deserve the name.
He every danger and fatigue would share,
His life when needed fearlessly expose;
He doubted not that they like hearts would bear,
To the same sacrifice their hearts dispose.
With sentiments like these — so just a cause —
They needs must conquer, win the world's applause,
And when their country free from war's alarms,
Return triumphant to her grateful arms.

Behold at sunset on that changeful day
The leaders, on those walls still mouldering there,
Near forty fathoms high above the bay,
Delighted scan a scene still wondrous fair.
Towards the south Seconnet's narrow tide,
Tinged with the splendors of the parting beams,
Where D'Estaing's frigates, decked with streamers, ride
Out to the yeasty foam where ocean gleams.
Beyond the turmoil of the wind-lashed wave

Mount Hope looms lurid in refracted rays,
Where once King Philip gave his life to save
His Wampanoags from stranger that betrays.
Far down that shore, were theirs the eagle's eye,
Point Judith, cradled in the storm-tost deep,
Lifts low its wrinkled front against the sky
Near where Canonicus, Canonchet, sleep.
In front, not far removed, on Quaker Hill,
Whose blood-drenched slope might name less peaceful bear,
The camps with war-worn tents the hollows fill;
And stars and stripes, and banner of the king,
The fleur-de-lis, their folds oft mingling fling
Upon the freshness of the evening air;
There the gay throng for morning's march prepared,
Cleansing their muskets, filling their canteens,
Or round the board their well-earned supper shared,
Then closed their eyelids upon earthly scenes.

The storm but lulled, not spent, recruits its strength
In sighs and sobs, the soldier's lullaby,
With all its earlier menace gained at length;
The darkling clouds sweep swiftly up the sky,
The stars go out as thickening scuds flew past,
A sable darkness shrouds the night in gloom
Save where flash low electric tongues of flame;

Nor still; for on the shores the billows boom,
From far away the muttering thunders came
And wilder, fiercer grew the angry blast.
Soon from above big pattering drops of rain
Splash on the canvas, now in streams descend;
The tents one moment glare, then dark again,
As deafening peals near by the welkin rend;
They flap and swirl, and all their fastenings strain,
Stakes, props, give way; they fall in hopeless wreck,
Crushing the sleepers. Yet some warriors bold
That elemental war but little reck,
All undisturbed 'mid perils of the night;
Some bruised or worse, and some from wet and cold,
Would gladly perish to escape their plight.
Two weary days of ceaseless wind and rain,
Sheltered by fence or barn, were whiled away.
While messengers their chiefs despatched again
For food, for ammunition, or for men
To fill their place who cared not longer stay;
Many mere volunteers to go and come
Sought safer shelter, hurrying to their home.
Still poured the rain; their three days' rations wet,
Their powder spoilt, their muskets specked with rust,
The sturdiest veteran well might chafe and fret,
That better days would come, might lose his trust.
Their troubled souls their leader sought to cheer,

Devised for every want its due relief,
In kindly words assured supplies were near,
Their great discomfort must of needs be brief;
These misadventures were the chance of war,
Their fortitude would reap its due reward,
Would make their glory and desert the more,
Foes be dismayed, their countrymen applaud;
The end attained, the future would recount
Their present hardships, and with equal pride
The dangers, toils, the conquerors surmount,
Their patient firmness whatsoe'er betide.

Before proceeding on their onward course
To learn the ground, reconnoissance in force
Pushed down the island, led by Livingston,
To near the outposts of the garrison.
From the high ground that overlooked each fort
And all the approaches to the guarded port,
Perchance some fleet upon the distant sea
Might tell if fleet of France were hovering near,
Or Howe or Byron in the offing be
At unexpected moment to appear.
But far as eye could range no ships in view
To affect the arrangements for the morrow's route;
His end accomplished, Livingston withdrew,
Each point examined by experienced scout.

In case the British general decides
Dispute their progress, seek by ambuscade
To take at disadvantage, Sullivan provides
That at each moment of their onward way
The army, or each separate brigade,
The whole or part, in order due displayed
To meet the enemy if inclined to fight;
And 'mid the tangle of the country farms
Commit the issue to the test of arms.

With the first sunshine all that proud array,
Their woes forgotten and their hopes elate,
With sturdy heart and tread pursue their way,
Their trust in Providence and not in fate.

From times remote two roads ran from the north,
Some distance from the shores, the island down,
Till at a smithy's forge they issued forth
To form a broader road towards the town.
The farms were fertile and the winds were strong,
With moss and lichen clad, high walls of stone
Extended miles these thoroughfares along,
Or cross the fields, to bound for each his own.
Each side from road to road the pioneers
Level these walls and open up the ground,
And on each flank a force each by-way clears,

All points of vantage in the region round.
No fleet at hand their progress on to haste,
They march with prudence, that the volunteers
Unused to burdens shall not vigor waste
That may be needed when the foe is near.

The van four of the noblest patriots led, —
Varnum and Greene and Glover and Cornell;
Though long since numbered with the honored dead,
Their worth and deeds their country's annals tell.
Greene, who commands his kinsman's own brigade,
With Prescott fought on Bunker's storied height,
With Arnold at Quebec, and late had made
Gallant defence of Redbank 'gainst the might
Of Donop and his host, four hundred slain;
Varnum, the best of soldiers, best of friends,
With every virtue and without a stain,
Sagacious statesman, able advocate;
Amphibious Glover fortune ever sends
To ferry troops imperilled to the main,
Trenton and Yorktown victories to gain,
This last where strife for independence ends.
The second line the generous Hancock guides
With Lovell, Whipple, Tyler, and Revere,
And near the centre the commander rides
To issue orders, — be, if needed, near.

Trumbull and Marshall, Lyman on his staff,
West closes up the march with the reserve,
While Livingston and Fleury and Laurens,
Who special praise for gallantry deserve,
Are everywhere that danger most impends;
Of the right wing upon the western road
Greene has the charge; of the left upon the east
The noble Lafayette, whose ardent veins
Heroic pulsed until their currents ceased.

That Saturday but six miles was their stent;
Headquarters, Sunday, Channing's loved abode;
Ere day was over they their course pursued,
Part in the fields, and part in either road.
Fort after fort they pass, still unopposed, —
All the more warily for this they went, —
Till, near the ground the hostile lines enclosed,
They pitch their tents and on their plans conclude.

CANTO IV

THE SIEGE.

WHERE Honeyman when raged the summer tide,
Berkeley's kind friend, was wont at times to dwell,
The hill that bears his name with lofty side
Served the besiegers for their citadel.
The advancing columns with the pick and spade
Throw up intrenchments near the hostile line
A league from Newport, where in mutual aid
The troops, hard pressed, may rally and combine
Should reinforcements to the enemy —
Events beyond control — compel retreat,
With lives so precious placed in jeopardy,
The cause itself endangered by defeat;
Not far away the frigates of the king
Command the crossing to the eastern shore,
From all the main-land could fresh forces bring,
Should aught untoward prove the need of more.

Gridley, who planned the works on Bunker Hill,
At Dorchester drove Howe to Halifax;

Who in his earlier youth helped Pepperell
Take Louisburg, the stronghold of the French;
Who naught of science or of genius lacks
To build the bastion or to run the trench;
With Crane, whose untaught engineering skill
Had often battered down the needed breach;
Accomplished Gouvion, chosen to instil
In Lafayette what Saxe and Vauban teach, —
With these for guides, but little chance to err,
Or be mistaken where they all concur.
Full seventy yards aloft from its broad brow,
Two miles away the ocean gleams and heaves,
'Twixt hill and sea lagoon more deep than now
Spreads to the beach and narrow passage leaves;
Two well-armed bastions this beach command,
With strong intrenchments the steep hillside crown,
The waste of life, to storm them would demand,
Dissuaded here assault upon the town;
Two lines of forts protect it farther north,
'Gainst which each night, under skilled engineers,
Thousands of men at twilight sallied forth
To build some work at morn complete appears,
Constructing covered ways and parallels,
Planting their mortars and their heavy guns,
Till day by day their incessant batter tells
The camp withdrawn, the approaching peril shuns.

Where now the smiling fields spread ripe with grain,
And graceful villas deck the scene around,
Fraternal hands the trampled herbage stain,
The hissing shells tear up the fertile ground.
Yet no great carnage marked their onward way,
Their leaders knew what signifies a life,
Their guns well aimed upon intrenchments play,
Trust to their reason to decide the strife,
Assured capitulation the result;
They were not of that sanguinary race
In wholesale slaughter with proud hearts exult.

When at the dawn of day the longed-for fleet,
Though shorn and shattered, loomed upon the view,
Americans its welcome advent greet,
Rejoiced at last their sanguine hopes come true.
Not so the garrison, — on whom, forlorn,
A deeper gloom the approaching vessels shed;
Their trusted works by batter rent and torn,
The fleet's return proclaims the doom they dread.
Straitened for food, their cattle scarce and poor,
Some rice was left, their meal was almost spent;
The fleet to fresh supplies would close the door,
The siege prolonged a cruel famine meant.
Convinced surrender near, they patient wait
The summons with content; and had D'Estaing,

As Nelson bold, as bravely risked his fate,
Won were his laurels, world with plaudits rang.
Greene, Lafayette on board, his aid besought,
Explained the progress then already made,
How diligently the patriot army wrought,
How wisely for success their plans were laid;
The town reduced, his fleet would safely ride
In Narragansett as Nantasket Roads,
Would he but for two days consent to bide,
Escaped the peril Byron's fleet forbodes.
Their prayers in vain, the Admiral disposed
His captains, urged the order of the king;
He might not stay while they were all opposed,
He hoped by land his troops in aid to bring.

The Sunday morn dawned dark with doubt and cares.
Byron or Howe might in those waters seek
The Admiral, fresh troops come unawares,
To escape in safety army prove too weak;
Not half its numbers disciplined in war,
Not fifteen hundred had in battle fought,
Our choicest youth their maiden weapons bore,
And even victory too dearly bought.
Most urgent missives, trusty messengers,
Were swiftly sent the land around for men,

Though the fond hopes that lately served to stir
Their patriot hearts had little influence then.
The chief his generals summoned to consult
What course 'mid such perplexities were best;
Of their deliberations the result,
Each what he thought wrote down at his request.
Greene, Glover, Varnum, Tyler, all concur
With Whipple: should the army all remain,
They should the raising of the siege defer,
And bolder front against the foe maintain;
All stores of value, not at once required,
Sent up the island or across the strait;
Before the army from the lines retired
They should with tranquil minds events await;
Perhaps some chance auspicious yet may show,
Without endangering troops we ill could spare,
How we might strike some unexpected blow
Should garrison from their intrenchments dare.
The attack most favored on the foes right flank,
Where at right angles beach and cliff connect,
Where heavy batteries along the bank
The town's approach from enemies protect.

Where now in summer's surf gay voices ring,
A happy throng of every age disport,
And yeasty breakers their refreshment bring,

Pointed the batteries of these hillside forts.
One, round about a mansion large and plain,
The home for generations of a race
Lords of the beach and all the vast domain,
Of whom the name still leaves some lingering trace;
Its outworks overhung the beetling crag
Now sloped and graded to a long decline;
The old beach-road then curled enough to drag
Sand-fish or sea-weed, or drive home the kine.
This fort, which formed the right of the defence,
Two miles or more removed from the attack,
The enemy might well place confidence
In its small guard to drive assailants back.
The plan proposed, — three hundred chosen men
Embark on Sachuest Beach by Paradise,
Land in some bay concealed along the cliff,
In fog or darkness the red house draw near,
And gathering on a hill existed then,
Trusting their bayonets the way would clear,
Each sentinel dispose of, forts surprise,
Three thousand veterans speed along the beach,
By signal rocket of success apprise,
In twenty minutes would the fortress reach;
Another rocket north of Tammany
Would breed confusion, and the moment shown
To press with vigor on the enemy, —

Newport would thus with ease become our own.
Cornell and Shepherd thought this project bold;
That when arrangements to withdraw complete,
They should march back, the northern earthworks
    hold
Till prudent from the island to retreat;
Yet in retiring tempt the British out,
Inflict upon them all we could of loss,
If at advantage possibly might rout,—
Arranged for each event the wisest course.
The disaffection of the German troops,
The noble Varnum thought, in open field
Would counterpoise our want of discipline,
With not unequal numbers triumph yield.
And sure such valiant gallant knights as he
Might snatch from multitudes the victory,
In doughty deed or quest of high emprise
For soldiership, with heroes share the prize;
No greed for fame, no dread of blame could swerve,
Sincere intentions prompted honest act;
Less caring to possess than to deserve
The good opinion generous souls attract;
Heedless of failure if the need should be,
Yet not admitting fate events directs,
With iron sceptre rules the universe;
No disappointment his strong will affects,

Glad to succeed, yet patient in reverse,
No doubt disturbs his philosophic soul,
What wise and proper all his life control.

With the last sail below the horizon's verge
Vanished all hope of winning back the town;
No arguments which they had left to urge
Could weigh against the orders of the Crown;
Their souls disheartened, so much labor lost,
Their scant resources wasted thus in vain, —
Not then the time to calculate the cost,
But strive each other's courage to sustain.
Panic, confusion, or disordered flight
Off of the island would be hopeless rout;
Their only safety, readiness to fight.
The siege was pressed from bastion and redoubt
With a bold front; whatever might impede
Their active movements should the foe come forth —
Cattle, artillery, all they did not need —
Was sent without delay towards the north;
Gridley despatched with pioneer and gun
To fortify their camp nine days before,
The lines at Bristol, works at Tiverton,
Construct, if he should think them needed more;
The task remained, should British fleet appear

With reinforcements to relieve the place,
To give his army courage, calm their fear,
That they in safety may their steps retrace.

Log-books jot down our progress o'er the deep,
The general orders, issued day by day,
Inform, direct, the army's record keep,
Spur on the bold and groundless fears allay.
While the ships lingered, might be entertained
Some hope D'Estaing would yield to their request;
Now that of this no single ray remained,
The minds of all grew bitter and depressed.
Anxious lest some such feeling of dismay
Should tempt the volunteers to leave the camp,
Knowing how much their purpose not to stay
The generous ardor of the others damp,
Sullivan, without concealment or reserve,
In fitting words to win their confidence,
Expressed what in his judgement best would serve
To inspire their breasts with healthier sentiments,
And thus his army in its toils preserve.

Deep his regret the sailing of the fleet
Should cast a shadow on his brave command;
We hoped with France the enemy defeat,

Supposed her aid we rightly might demand.
But they were much deceived who should suppose
Our force in peril, that they chose to go;
The British force the opposing lines enclose,
Our number to their own superior know.
So long as bravely glows each manly breast
With patriot ardor, with its sacred flame,
No part the island which we now possessed
We need give up, unless some squadron came;
Not in an instant such events take place,
Our scouts watch for their coming along shore,
We from the offing can their progress trace,
Anticipate their coming long before
Time will be requisite to reach the port,
To furl their sails, to drop their anchors down,
To disembark their troops, the lines to reach
In numbers that were equal to our own.
Every event that possibly can chance
Has been considered preparations made
Even to retreat without precipitance
Should prudence to a prompt retreat persuade.
With great surprise your General has learned
That many volunteers propose to leave,
And throw away the honors they have earned,—
A lasting proof their imperilled country give
Of want of firmness and of bravery.

With all despatch against the garrison
The approaches will be pressed with vigor on;
He knows the value to America
Of the brave officers, soldiers, citizens,
Whom now he has the honor to command;
She shall not by rash step of his incur
The slightest risk of sacrificing men
Whose safety is important to the land;
Let them but place implicit confidence
In their commander, upon whom devolves
This sacred charge, under kind Providence,
Which in its wisdom what shall come resolves.
He feels assurance the event will show
Americans by their own arms obtain
What their allies refuse them help to gain.

Truth may be bitter, yet still opportune
Balm to the angry mood provoked by wrong;
Rankling, it reached its mark, and D'Estaing soon
Promised to come forthwith, four thousand strong.
The orders not addressed to rank and file,
But read to officers of each brigade,
Were not designed their allies to revile,
But in the crisis, soldiers reconcile
To fight their fight without the promised aid.
Deserters, feigned, came from the town as spies

To learn what said, intended, planned, or thought;
Pigott admits he could no means devise
To obtain the information that he sought.
These wingèd words, passed on from tent to tent,
The brave encouraged, but the weak dismayed;
Conveyed to angry minds much more than meant.
Few but believed that they had been betrayed;
Both Lafayette and Fleury, well aware
How quick their countrymen to take offence,
Urged that his words interpretation bear
Significance far other than their sense.
Though feeling what he said was justified,
Unwilling to refuse such faithful friends,
With their request the General complied,
Thus two days later sought to make amends.

Removed his heavier guns, secured his stores,
An easy, safe retreat in case of need,
Before a succoring fleet could reach these shores,
Compel us quit positions that we hold,
All of the island, any part, concede,
He had reason to believe the French, returned,
In its reduction would with us proceed,
The honor of its conquest jointly earned.
Great his surprise, by friends he valued, told

His previous orders thought to intimate
Departure of the fleet, showed fixed design
No more to help us in our enterprise.
Ungenerous, illiberal minds assign
Interpretations not a word implies
To what he said in orders of that day.
He would not leave least color to malign;
Not his to know the instructions of the king,
Determine if the French obliged to go;
His only wish that favoring winds might bring
Them back, with us to strike the final blow,
Attention and regard our compact pay,
Add to the obligations that we owe,
Their constant acts of kindness on us lay,
Throughout the contest from its earliest day,
At this propitious time their friendship show.
He would once more express his deep regret
Many refuse to stay are free to go,
And at this time, most critical, forget
The sacrifices we our country owe.
They err, assume that nothing can be done
Unless by siege, our object to effect;
Our force outnumbers still the garrison;
Let all that may, before too late, reflect
Such as await with patience the event,
Whatever course the wisest to pursue

The island to reduce, and stay content,
Will win most credit, to the cause be true.

While hopes delusive smiled, the waverers, stirred
By generous ardor, still content to stay;
Three neighbors of the chief, the attack deferred,
Approach at night the sentinels, unheard,
Two badly wound, and yet another slay;
The alarum sounds, and to the rescue rush
An Anspach outpost near, who, on the alert,
Familiar with the ground their quarry flush,
Escape cut off, and capture them unhurt;
Another force, when venturing too near
To Fanning's quarters, like disaster met;
While Hessians, foraging devoid of fear,
Found themselves prisoners, but with feigned regret;
Tired of constant toil and scanty fare,
Disgusted with the cause for which they fought,
Strong, fierce to fight, of peerless hardihood,
They felt the shame of being sold and bought.
Chafing as slaves, in such close prison pent,
With aught that eased such galling chains content,
If our new levies had to war been trained,
If all our troops been veteran like the rest,
Against such lukewarm foes Newport were gained,
The tyrant's tread no more the country pressed.

Three British ships on Thursday gain the port,
The harbingers of hundreds on the way;
Three thousand men, their patience spent, report
Their intent to quit the camp at break of day.
The chief well knew what effort it had cost
To bring his troops equipped so far afield,
How grieved the country at such efforts lost,
If ground so bravely won compelled to yield;
Troubled, yet not depressed, one effort more:
Turning to Lafayette, his faithful friend,
Besought him speed to Boston and implore
D'Estaing at once four thousand troops to send,
That they might thus the northern forts retain
And, reinforced, the land now lost regain.

The gallant marquis, generous as brave,
Required no urgent prayer to mount his steed;
Rode seventy miles in seven hours to save
The cause his own now in its direst need.

In consultation as the day went on,
Aware each shifting breeze might bring a fleet,
Their numbers then less than the garrison,
To make more difficult their safe retreat,
The generals reluctantly decide,
All circumstances justified been done,

The works still pressed, the enemy defied,
Their preparations make at set of sun;
Without confusion when the night set down,
Leaving no spoil to glut the foeman's pride,
Their progress unmolested from the town,
The island's length their phantom forces glide
For five short hours; when on the sloping side
Of Butts's Hill they lay them down to rest,
And sleep, well earned, the slumbers of the blest.

CANTO

THE BATTLE.

AT flush of morn, to Hessians on the wall
    The scene looked strange, and no reveille beat,
No stir or morning gun, but, silent, all
Doubt what portends, or battle or retreat;
The sergeant of the guard to council called,
They soon concluded to apprise the chief.
Sir Robert came, not wholly unappalled,
No ships yet signalled with the hoped relief;
But when the sun displayed its welcome disk,
And all betokened the besiegers gone,
His duty clear, whatever were the risk,
To learn without delay what should be done,
He ordered Prescott cross the narrow strand
To send a regiment from his second line,
To flank the rebels' left, for Brown's command
Should occupy the abandoned works assign;
Smith's five battalions speedily pursue
Along the eastern road the flying foe;
Along the west the Hessian chasseurs flew;
Voit and Seaboth's Anspach soldiers speed,

Under Losberg at double-quick proceed,
To annoy the retreating rebels as they go.

The course that Pigott took not unforeseen,
When morning's dawn their midnight march betrayed,
Sullivan posts an ample force between
The town and where his slumbering army rest;
Livingston's light corps, selected from the best,
Three miles in front of where the army laid,
Guarded the eastern road 'gainst Smith's brigade;
Laurens with Henry Talbot block the west;
In rear of both the picket under Wade.
In force sufficient, should be need for aid,
Or wiser deemed their forces to unite,
A corps despatched this object to attain
That they might with the more advantage fight.
'T is said at early morn begun the fight
Closed with the bayonet charge before the night.
Talbot, of race not backward in the fray,
Charged on the Hessian horse two leagues from town,
Pushing upon the west their upward way,
Driving them back disordered on their own,
The brave Laurens, with his selected force,
From every knoll and wall a galling fire
Poured out on front and flank of man and horse,

Then, as concerted, farther back retire.
Smith on the right, hearing the volleys roar
One half the Twenty-second sends in aid, —
Campbell, and since McCullum More,
What scion of his brave and gallant stock
Such call to duty ever disobeyed,
Or met reluctantly the battle's shock?

Beyond where Channing dwelt in pious love
For human kind of every tint and land,
A broad domain of pasture, field, and grove
In part still sacred to his Lord's command,
Crossed from the east to west a narrow lane,
And from that cross-road opened yet a fourth
Bounding with massive walls a field of grain,
With broken surface rising to the north;
Behind these walls, with here and there a gap,
Wade part his picket placed in ambuscade,
That there he might the enemy entrap;
Laurens or Livingston, if needed, aid.
Campbell with quickening footsteps pressing on
To help the Germans fighting on the left,
His column turning from the early sun,
Plunged rank on rank into the narrow cleft
All unsuspecting, as along the road,
Behind these walls above their heads concealed,

Sharpshooters fire and speedily reload,
And ere their peril to the rear revealed,
Wrapped in the smoke aloft, from off the bank
Make havoc of their crowded, helpless foes,
Pouring their bullets into rear and flank,
Surprised, disordered, by these unseen blows.
Incensed, provoked, the British climb the slope;
The walls were high, deadly the rifles' aim;
The battle surges off, since vain to cope
With marksmen slew all in their vision came.
One fourth the British fell no more to rise;
More blest who killed outright, than wounded dies.

In battle trained, Pigott's quick ear detects
Its shifting tide; scouts tell him what occurs;
Fanning's Provincials he at once collects,
Sends to relieve the beaten-back chasseurs;
Thus reinforced, they gathered all their strength
And press Laurens, who steadily withdraws.
Driven from one redoubt, he gains at length
Another breastwork farther up the shores;
Here for a while he more than held his own,
Though ardent his desire to attack,
Then, ordered by his chief, fell fighting back,
His march with bleeding foemen strown;
The lady bright whose spouse for freedom fought,

And through the siege remained within the town,
Tells us what crowds of wounded soldiers brought,
Fearing to find among the rest her own.

The combat thickens; all along the lines
Pigott speeds reinforcements to the front,
The Fifty-fourth and part of Brown's and Huyn's
To Smith, who on the right now bears the brunt.
Smith sends him word the foes on Quaker Hill
Its southern slopes with solid masses fill;
Sullivan had despatched, to help his own,
One regiment to Laurens, one to Livingston,
With orders to fall back, yet fighting still,
To the main force, which they effect with skill.
Greene's first advice, to leave the ground they held
And fight the battle where this contest fought;
But the new levies in the force compelled
More prudent counsel upon second thought;
If not in strength with thrice their numbers cope,
Or hold for long the whole right wing at bay
Like a fierce bloodhound at a tiger's throat,
The light corps still their onward progress stay.
At length, as reinforcements reached the ground,
And Sullivan called Livingston away,
Smith pushing boldly on before him, found
Glover's sea-veterans ready to attack,

Who charged his serried mass and many slew.
Both sides fought bravely, or to gain or keep,
As breast to breast they struggled on the steep.

Fierce was the onslaught; Smith, forced slowly back,
Behind the lines of Quaker Hill withdrew;
Losberg, his Germans worsted, weary, worn,
Harassed by Laurens since the early morn,
Rejoiced at last to find a moment's rest
Where Anthony and Turkey, sides and crest,
Extend their ridges to the north and west.
In front, half league away, on Butts displayed,
Sullivan marshalled his five thousand men,
Reserves a thousand yards behind, arrayed
Near Howland's Ferry, which he meant to cross
Should chance the British fleet, expected then,
Expose his army to too serious loss.
Right of his front and nearer to the bay,
Armed with large guns, stood a strong bastion
To guard his flank and drive all ships away,
With one stanch regiment for its garrison.
Between the hostile lines a meadow land,
With scattered trees and copse in valleys spread,
Where soon fierce foemen, fighting hand to hand,
Each other's blood in copious streamlets shed.

About three hours to noon, when all was still,
A booming gun pealed from the British right;
Its echoes lost as forth from hill to hill
Responsive batteries ushered in the fight;
From either army skirmishers thrown out
Like skilful swordsmen in some deadly fray,
In feint and thrust and parry turned and closed,
Cautious alike no vital point exposed;
Each strives his foe, when off his guard, to slay,
So now the combatants by every wile,
The other from the cover of his guns
Endeavored by some stratagem beguile;
Sullivan, hoping some advantage gain,
Tempting his enemy to the open plain
Towards the ferry, or to quit the isle.

Midst clouds of smoke that darkened all the skies,
Two ships of war and smaller craft appear;
Crane, all too shrewd and wary for surprise
As to effect their object they drew near,
His heavy guns from two masked batteries
Drove off afar their useless cannonade,
Designed, our flanks exposed, to enfilade,
As, under cover of these guns afloat,
The British meant to cut off our retreat;

They now their thoughts and all their might devote
To take these batteries their plans defeat.

Down Anthony, with strong and rapid sweep,
British and Hessians push for the redoubt,
But little glory win, advantage reap;
From Greene they met resistance firm and stout;
Greene, Varnum, Glover, Cornell, wise and brave,
Stemmed the massed torrent in its onward rush,
Slowly but sternly turned the mighty wave,
Then part by part its several fragments crush;
Here, side by side, lay sixty British dead,
There thirty Hessians slain not far away,
The emerald turf about with carnage red, —
Men stricken down who had not time to pray.
Disordered, disarranged, in helpless rout,
The foemen rallied at their leader's call,
And, trained to war, they briskly turn about,
Regain their lines and into order fall.
Disheartened, not dismayed, more caution taught,
Their comrades slain inflame their souls with wrath;
Field batteries, with dire destruction fraught,
To their revenge are brought to clear the path.
This was a game at which both sides could play;
Our own artillerists well their lesson knew, —

Wherever quivering leaves approach betray,
The shells and shrapnel on their errand flew.

Again sweep down with more discretion led,
Hessians, resolved this time the outwork take,
Off to their left towards the water spread,
Nor know what danger lurks in every brake;
To enslave their brethren, Briton's purchased braves,
Germans and Indians to destroy and spoil,
Led on by Ward, our manumitted slaves
Helped much that day the British plan to foil.
Posted behind a thicket in the vale,
Thrice down the slope the Hessians on them charge;
The sable warriors ply their shot like hail,
Gap upon gap in Hessian ranks enlarge;
So many wounded and so many slain,
The German Colonel urged his men in vain;
Convinced at last no effort would avail,
He marched them to the trenches back again,
The next day seeking, so we're told the tale,
To exchange commands, lest, if his own retained,
Of his own men he should be made the targe.

With hearts cast down and garments stained with
    gore,
With ranks that tell of many comrades dead,

Existence sweet the thought of all before,
Of wife and child whom they may see no more,
Well might the bravest breast inspire with dread.
War is a sport that plays with human lives
To please the vanity or glut the greed;
Little care kings how many widowed wives,
How many better men in battle bleed,
So long as victory perch upon their side,
And others' misery gratify their pride;
The conquest theirs, for them the laurels claimed;
For officers' promotion or disgrace,
And best and bravest oft unjustly blamed;
Pensions make slight amends for soldiers maimed;
The winning nation in the bloody race
Finds freedom bartered for mere pelf and place;
Still where the cause to cast such thraldom off,
To win for ages liberty and law,
Power may contemn, its myrmidons may scoff,
Mankind, enfranchised, justifies the war.
For no such cause did Hess or Briton fight,
But to subject to an unwilling yoke
A gallant people battling for their right,
For sacred compacts their oppressors broke.

No time was lost; reorganized, their force
In all its strength arrayed, descends the hills,

Its left towards the fort directs its course,
Its right the valley by Seconnet fills.
With prudent caution led, and steady tread,
Each breast with generous resentment fired,
Their bold array might well have filled with dread
Foes by less sacred sentiments inspired.
From all the crests the angry cannons roar,
Reverberating round from every shore;
Their iron missiles, hurtled through the smoke,
Upon the advancing mass their havoc pour;
As midst its ranks the shells in fragments broke,
Men stagger, fall, are carried to the rear.

The enemy advance, and rebels near
Halt, aim, and fire, and speedily reload,
And then again with quickened footsteps move,
The ground beneath their feet with dead men strowed
By skilful marksmen, who each chance improve
To lay them low as proudly on they strode.
As now in fuller view they reach the base
Of the steep slopes on which the rebels stand,
Deploy in lines as if upon parade,
Fire, and load at foemen close at hand;
Both armies front to front and face to face,
The hostile lines upon the mead below,
Through the dense smoke but sorry marksmen
  make;

The Americans the slope and distance know,
Their balls of death their course appointed take;
The stricken ranks, disordered and appalled
Must needs have fallen into rout again,
When "Close your ranks, push on!" each captain
  called,
Nor midst the crash of battle heard in vain.
Renewed their ardor, they their chiefs obey,
Speeding their steps, for so the danger less,
Climb the steep hill-side, on with vigor press,
Yet ever find Greene's veterans in their way;
The well-served batteries down their comrades mow,
The withering musketry shrivels like a scroll;
They frantic rush to give back blow for blow,
While every volley other death-knells toll.
As hungry wolves that raven for their food,
Infuriate lioness plundered of her whelp,
With desperate valor and with purpose fell,
With bayonets fixed, some trust in sword and ball,
In one vast compact mass, with shout and yell
They gain the heights and on the rebels fall.

Vain beats the sea against the rooted rock.
With weapons ready and with mind composed
The patriots dauntless met the coming shock,
And with their foes in mutual slaughter closed.

It was a desperate struggle, and both sides
Lost heavily the men they least could spare;
Death on the smoke, his palest courser, rides,
And many nobly die who nobly dare.
The gallant Varnum, valiant paladin,
Lost largest in the thickest of the fray,
But the like courage all the line displayed;
Cornell's, and Glover's, and Greene's own brigade
Though hotly pressed, still resolute to win,
Hold fast the British veterans at bay,
Whose furious onsets, when repulsed, renewed.
With little hope most clearly signified,
Their main design their leaders still pursued.
For as in front attention occupied,
The key to the position that they sought
Was not so much a victory over Greene,
As seize the water batteries and fort,
Which guard our right and all the space between,
Hold at safe distance all their guns afloat
On which they trust to cut off our retreat,
And which these batteries kept too far remote
To harm, unless arrived the expected fleet.

The combat thickened, every officer
Kept well in hand the soldiers that he led,
Who to his will implicitly defer,

On him rely till life's last drop be shed.
Each but a part of one grand, perfect whole,
All guided by one judgment, on one plan,
Whose quick conceptions all the rest control,
The general movement, individual man,
As proved the event though oft the ranks disturbed,
At times confused the orderly array,
Each his own men, when too impulsive, curbed,
Or animates as mingled in the fray;
As bloodhounds leashed, impatient to be loosed,
Their thoughtful leaders cautious not to waste
One single life that can be safely spared,
No end imperilled by untempered haste,
Officers and men the common danger shared.
Indeed, while raged this struggle on the hill,
The Hessians on the west the fort assail
In so great numbers, such determined will,
It seemed as if such efforts must avail.

The General all the issues of the fight
With thoughtful yet with tranquil mind observed,
Knows well the moment to put forth his might,
And speeds a regiment, for such chance preserved,
Of Continentals, veterans in war,
Who oft before had borne the battle's brunt,
And ardent, fresh, around the hill-side wind
With needed succor, to the struggling front.

Reposing from their vigils of the night
In the cool shadows of the sheltering hill,
While on its sunny slopes thus raged the fight,
Livingston and his vanguard slumbered still.
No battle's roar disturbed them as they slept,
Unconsciously his clutch upon his sword;
As tired hound in sleep pursues the chase,
Or baited bull the horse and rider gores,
His fitful dreams his morning fights retrace,
His hard-pressed ranks to order due restores;
Then his loved Hudson o'er his vision creeps,
His distant wife clings fond to his embrace,
Or sits in lonely silence, smiles and weeps,
Or for his safety Providence implores.
As thus his limbs their lusty strength renew,
His comrades share in his well-earned repose;
The healthy blood in wonted courses flew,
The patriot breast with generous ardor glows;
And when the summons calls them to the front,
Each from his lair, equipped, with vigor leapt,
Each to his post with proud elation stept
And rushed, refreshed, to bear the battle's brunt.

These roused, his left Sullivan timely sent
To assail the right flank of the enemy,
By their impetuosity enmeshed,

Yet pressing west towards the battery;
Then all that August noon, of kindred race
Both armies, by experienced generals led,
In that contracted vale and narrow space,
With dauntless resolution fought and bled.
The cannonade still thundering on the hill
To help their own, the enemy dismay,
The guns afloat with ineffective fire,
Dun with its pall of smoke, the welkin fill,
And crackling muskets solemn requiem play
As men, shot down, with bitter groans expire.
The British ships, deluded, near the shore,
Their heavy broadsides batter on the fort;
Our batteries respond with fiercer roar
Till, pierced and rent, the ships can do no more,
And safer mooring in the distance sought.
The sable troops still hold their wooded knoll
Where Hessians slain lay weltering in their gore;
From sea to sea incessant volleys roll
From the Seconnet, where the Grenadiers
On raw recruits their heavy onslaught bore,
Along the slopes where Butts its summit rears,
And Smith and Greene their angry battle waged,
Off to the bay where Losberg fumed and raged
To take the fort beside the western shore.
That torrid noon, that crowded battle-field

Unfanned by breezes, unrefreshed by rain,
No time for rest their constant movements yield.
Soldiers athirst for water thirst in vain;
The martinets of England stiffly clad,
Their allies for parade and less for war,
All that long day but slight refreshment had;
In haversack each man his rations bore,
Their moistening drops the canteens yield no more.
The rustic patriots cast their coats aside
And fight the battle with their limbs left free,
Their scant supplies brought over on the tide;
They need not much, their lives in jeopardy;
Weary, enhungered, not for them to care
So long as they the victory may gain,
Content if Providence their lives shall spare,
Or, if the cause demands, not spent in vain.
The stream that gurgles through yon neighboring
    glade
From tramp of busy feet ran turbid then,
Its heated flow nor feverish thirst allayed,
Nor soothed the anguished brows of dying men;
The lurid sun, through canopies of smoke,
Glowed like a furnace on their aching sense,
And sulphurous fumes and dusty vapors choke
The few last moments left for penitence;
Yet no regrets their passing moments cloud, —

Death for their country, death for freedom's cause,
The smoke of battle for their honored shroud,
A grateful nation, and the world's applause
Are all they ask as, sinking to their rest,
Their eyes refreshed reopen on the blest.

Long sorely pressed, at last Greene forces back
The restless swarm, that strives and strives again
To find some point more vulnerable to attack;
As oft repulsed, and all their struggles vain,
No marvel that the sturdiest spirit droops
Amidst such strife, such suffering and toil;
The most intrepid of the hostile troops
Waver, fall back from charge, again recoil,
Four rebel regiments now hold in check
Their further onslaughts. Another, trained to war,
Swoops here and there upon their hopeless wreck
Where least expected; there it smites them sore.

Against our left Pigott his whole reserves
Paraded on the slopes of Quaker Hill;
As now in peril his best troops observes
Against superior forces struggling still,
He sends adown the slope with quickened tread
The last battalions that he had, to aid
The troops that will not fly, yet stand in dread.

Sullivan bids Lovell, with his stanch brigade
From Massachusetts, this column's progress block,
Strike flank and front; while his artillery played
Till they drew back, unequal to the shock.
While Sullivan orders Colonel Livingston,
Who on that day the brightest laurels won,
With Jackson's regiment that at Monmouth fought
And at Slate Hill that morn the fight began,
To take position farther to the west,
Await events, decide upon his plan,
And, should occur the happy moment sought,
With unexpected onset, bayonets charged,
Rush double-quick upon the troops depressed
In the low land, in narrow bounds compressed,
And drive them from the valley to their fort.
The men, confiding in their noble chief
Who leads, not follows, when by foes beset,
Swept briskly on the enemy, surprised,
Who, driven at bay, fought bravely hand to hand,
But overpowered, helpless of relief,
At every point of vantage made a stand;
The turf with blood all slippery and wet,
Their ranks disordered and demoralized,
They yield the ground, and then, ashamed, come
    back,
To give up all for lost, unwilling yet.

To rally them their officers strive in vain;
They lose not courage, but the sinews lack
With such fresh forces to contend again.
Pressed cross the valley, up the hill-side pressed,
They hurry to the cover of their guns;
One battery their swift pursuers get,
Which their commanders in their flight forget, —
One trophy of this charge of Livingston's.

This vigorous charge had turned the battle's tide,
Helped, too, to turn the balanced tide of war;
Not wholly routed, yet with humbled pride
Sense of defeat speeds fast from shore to shore;
Right wing and left the enemy retreat,
And up the hill-sides glide with rapid feet;
What could be done to harass as they went
Was not neglected, but their covert near,
Though prudence to their flight fresh vigor lent,
Such veterans could but little know of fear.

It was near night — Van Matsburg says but four —
Four hours since noon when thus the combat ends,
Pronounced the best-fought battle of the war,
So Lafayette its generals commends.
Sullivan, fain those strong intrenchments storm,
Knew well his troops fatigued, nor cared expose,

To doubtful issues, regiments that form
The nation's chief dependence 'gainst its foes.
Since Friday's dawn his men upon their feet
In marches, preparation, or in fight,
Could hardly hope an equal force defeat;
Thus strongly posted before came the night,
He still indulged the hope the Admiral,
Moved by the urgent prayers of Lafayette,
Would send his troops, or his own earnest call
For reinforcements might be answered yet.
Pigott, expecting soon five thousand men
With Clinton and his formidable fleet,
Had little wish to renew the combat then;
But when at dusk the rebels by the bay
Surround the chasseurs to cut off retreat,
Huyn's, Fanning's corps were ordered in support;
A smart engagement drove them soon away
To Butts' Hill, near by their strengthened fort;
With little vigor to fight more that day,
The weary men regain their several lines,
Posting their pickets near their enemy's;
And when came off the sea the evening breeze,
The crescent moon beyond the bay declines,
Each army on their arms their slumbers take,
Prepared for battle when the morning break.

When the reveille sounds, the combatants
Flock to their ranks, expecting to be led
Against intrenchments bristling with their guns,
And little cared how soon their blood were shed;
For sense of danger but invigorates
The human breast that knows no craven fear,
Content the life kind Providence creates
Is His to take or spare when danger near;
Enough for them to know their duty there
By conduct, courage, to subdue the foe;
And for the coming strife both sides prepare
To strike or parry the impending blow.
They profit by the lessons yester taught,
With equal numbers, valor, arms, and skill,
Even victory by storming dearly bought
Where works well planned, as those on either hill.
Each hopes to tempt the other to attack,
Each resolute by no deceit provoked
To expose their forces to be driven back;
Pigott expects, besides the promised fleet,
Sullivan, the army Lafayette invoked,
Nor chose impair his chance of safe retreat
By being crippled, should he not defeat.

Scanning with constant watchfulness his foe
Lest it should make some unexpected spring,

His general orders gave his men to know
What joy their country the event would bring;
No usual phrase could fittingly express
His pleased delight, as yesterday he viewed
His gallant army, in the battle's press
Exhibit such heroic fortitude.
All thanks to Greene, his generals, each brigade,
Who long and bravely bore alone the brunt,
To Lovell and his officers, whose aid
Whose dauntless intrepidity dismayed,
And helped repulse, the enemy in front,
With their great strength in equal combat strove,
Then off the field of action, routed, drove.
Laurens and Livingston claim their warmest thanks
As their artillerists, Crane and Gouvion,
Whose well-served guns distressed the hostile ranks,
Shielded our own as they went moving on.
Troops not in battle actually concerned,
In courage vied with those the foe attacked,
To take their part with equal ardor burned;
Would share their laurels, but occasion lacked.
Profoundly grateful for the victory won,
One sacred duty still for them remains, —
To inter their dead, in action nobly fell,
With all the honors such a death-bed gains.
Our wounded comrades, too, deserve their care;

Whatever for their comfort can procure,
Effort or cost, to effect their speedy cure,
Who had the charge, were ordered not to spare.

While thus employed in binding up the wounds,
Paying due homage to the honored slain,
A parley from the outer picket sounds,
And Campbell pleads, nor pleads his cause in vain;
Decoyed in ambush where the by-ways crossed,
His regiment the yester morn had lost
One fourth its strength, yet on with vigor pressed,
And in the desperate struggle with the rest
Long held their ground disputed breast to breast.
He came to seek among the mingled dead
His sister's son, who in this later strife
Had fallen by his side, a hero bred,
For king and country early gave his life.

Still hopeful of good tidings from the north
That on their way march all the troops of France,
To throw away their strong position loath,
The hours of that Sabbath-day advance,
When from the ferry, speeded in hot haste,
Despatches reach the chief from Washington,
That Clinton and his host no moments waste,
With every favoring breeze are pressing on.

He forthwith orders workmen to the lines,
Disguised the intent to cross from off the isle,
Prepares for battle till the day declines;
The tents are pitched still better to beguile.
Meantime, our batteries along the shore
Keep at safe distance all the British ships,
As, screened by hills from view, in frequent trips
The sick and wounded, cattle, gun, and store,
Boats passing to and fro in safety bore.
As the respective sentinels alert
Mark every sight and sound with quickened sense,
The opposing guards a hundred yards apart,
This thorough preparation for defence
Diverts suspicion with consummate art
From aught that might be thought but a pretence.
But when the sun and moon had gone to rest,
The stars alone emit their feeble light,
And sentinels their beats in silence pressed,
Issuing from their tents upon the night,
Five thousand men move back of Butts' Hill
Down to the ferry, and are pulled acrost,
All in such order, with such care and skill
That not a life or aught of value lost.
Amphibious Glover, who at Brooklyn saved
Our troops, environed both by land and sea,
Across the Delaware, with ice-floes paved,

Steered our brave men to Trenton's victory;
Again this night with Cornell, Lafayette,
Who twenty leagues had rode in six short hours, —
With vigor left they all fatigue forget, —
Preserved from toils these precious troops of ours;
And just in time, for as their anxious chief
With his life-guard still lingered on the shore,
The foe, aroused, with preparations brief
Around the hills in solid columns pour,
And as the latest guardsman reached the boat,
A few their volleys wounded while afloat.

The night's fatigue had won its needed rest;
When morning came the troops upon parade,
To their commanders Sullivan addressed
His parting words, his dispositions made:
Congratulations, that without the loss
Of gun or store, of officers or men,
They stood unharmed upon the main again,
From off the island safely all withdrawn;
This, though the enemy's opposing force,
From various intelligence, well known,
Superior in numbers to his own.
Their ships of war controlled the neighboring bay,
And had we waited for another dawn
Must have at disadvantage fought our way.

Such a retreat thus regularly made
Without confusion, carried out as planned,
The zeal by men and officers displayed
Reflected honor on his whole command.
To his own staff, to Trumbull, Sherburne, Long,
Russell and Sullivan who volunteer,
His unreserved acknowledgments belong
For faithful service, spirited and brave.
Brave Gouvion and every engineer
Whose skill and industry no task could tire
In building batteries and approaches near
To Newport, by their well-directed fire
Compelled their foes within their lines retire;
Well merited the praise he gladly gave.
To the light corps dissolved, now all restored
To their respective posts, his warmest thanks
With pride he would their valiant deeds accord,
Both those that led and those that filled the
    ranks.
Nor in conclusion could he well refrain
Expressing obligations to Cornell,
Whipple, and Olney for their thoughtful care
In passing guns and luggage from the main;
And more remiss, if he should fail to tell
With what devoted zeal and oversight
They had embarked the troops the previous night.

The sick and wounded when their state admits
Would be removed to Providence, and there
Receive the treatment that the place permits, —
Physicians' skill and nurses' tender care.
The right wing cantoned 'long the western shore
Greene to command, the left wing Lafayette,
Glover his own brigade and Jackson's corps
The centre line stationed at Providence,
With Lovell's, Titcomb's, near at Pawtucket;
Tyler at Warwick, Doggett's regiments,
One at Fall River, at Slade's Ferry one;
Cornell retain his post at Tiverton,
Varnum at Warren near his natal place,
And Christopher Greene, brave hero of Redbank,
At Fishkill three years later vilely slain,
To take position on the southern flank
At Greenwich, home of his illustrious race.

The Continentals and militia gone,
The whole a scanty force to guard and keep
One hundred miles against an active foe,
Ten thousand strong that formed the garrison,
Who well might strike some unexpected blow
Should those that watch them fold their hands in
    sleep.
That very morn Sir Clinton's promised fleet,

Its fourscore ships and troops five thousand men,
From round Point Judith up the harbor beat
And all the sea-girt isle is theirs again.
Our well-aimed batteries had left their trace,
Breach upon breach the heavy balls had rent;
Great his surprise to find so weak the place,
To the besieged his courteous compliment.

For yet another year King George's flag
Waved in its pride from fort and battlement,
While watchful sentinels on hill and crag
Maraud or raid upon its farms prevent.
The British ships their cruel vengeance wreak
On many a town exposed along the shore;
Wherever were beheld defences weak
Their floating batteries church and dwelling tore.
Falmouth and Fairfield, to the east and west,
The brand completes the havoc of the gun,
The folk dismayed could find no moment's rest,
Nor cared repair the ruthless havoc done.

When Pigott left to Prescott the command
A galley bore his name and guards the bay
Along the eastern shore, not near the land
Lest Compton's batteries drive their ship away.
Many the laurelled wreath the battle wove,

Not one more signal bravery displayed
Than Silas Talbot, who that morning strove
With Laurens, who fell later in the war;
Fleury, who scars from that encounter bore
To mark with blood each step the Hessians made;
His gallant deeds upon the neighboring seas
Had frequent prizes won when needed most,
Rich freighted vessels trembled lest the breeze
Should waft to spoil the terror of the coast.
Byron at Boston blockading D'Estaing
The Pigott galley unsuspecting lay
When, watching for his chance, in darkness sprang
The dauntless Talbot on his helpless prey,
With threescore heroes to such service bred.
From Prudence in a light-armed vessel dropped,
Passed Bristol Ferry with all canvas spread,
In Mt. Hope Bay the favoring hazes wrapped;
Till drifting down at night Seconnet's tide,
By Fogland Ferry and its hostile guns,
Under bare poles along the Compton side,
All observation from the sentries shuns,
His boat upon the ebb with muffled oar
Gropes till it hears the galley's midnight hail
When, veiled in mist, the "Hawk" with rapid wing,
Borne by the breeze come rushing through the fog,
Pouncing upon the galley with a spring,

That with its eight twelve-pounders lays a-log.
Fastening his grapples, Talbot and his crew
Break through the boarding nettings to the deck,
The drowsy Britons from their hammocks flew,
Nor knew what ill impended, fire or wreck.
Driven below, the hatches soon were fast,
Her brave commander left alone to fight;
A contest so unequal could not last,
And ere the morning dawn brought back the light,
The captors with their prize, thus sleeping caught,
Entered in triumph some near friendly port,
Nor many nights before the galley lay
The watch-dog of the rebels in the bay.

CANTO VI.

IROQUOIS.

MEANWHILE D'Estaing, his orders to obey,
　　His fleet refits, and watching for his chance
Storm drives the beleaguering ships away,
Or they went roving round to raid or slay,
Sails to the south his twenty ships of France.
Granada, St. Lucie, his gloomy soul
Racked with regret, restored his tireless zeal.
In tropic seas his ships triumphant roll,
For Newport lost, his wounds, still rankling, heal.
When from Nantasket Roads he issued forth
His hope and promise, when the spring should come,
With his strong fleet and force returning North,
To aid his allies if not ordered home.

For near two centuries France and England strove
Which should possess this mighty continent,
And when, at last, the conquering British drove
Her rivals off, a feverish discontent
Envenoming both minister and king,
Encouragement our disaffection lent,

Their Eden lost, to fresh subjection bring.
The cross the Catholics planted at Quebec,
Port-Royal, Castine, and beyond the roar
Of grand Niagara, saint and savage deck
With the like unction as the years before,
Down to the Gulf its banners once unrolled;
The Indian loved the French who fish and hunt,
Hating the English who his birthplace hold
And with imperious sway his pride affront.

The Admiral's promise when he left the coast,
Prompted by Lafayette then going home,
To sanguine souls appeared no idle boast
Were they prepared when the right moment come.
Congress and Washington forthwith decide
To wait with patience the long-wished-for hour,
Their troops to discipline and food provide,
Holding in check the king's superior power.
The land, exhausted, had scant means or arms
To assail the enemy behind his walls,
But patriot's breast no craven thought alarms,
No odds a soul like gallant Wayne's appalls;
His chosen men, at night, at Stony Point
The fortress scale and capture guns and men,
The copious streams of blood the fields anoint,
With little loss regained their post again.

Like their fierce allies, in their cruel raid
Britons spared neither child nor woman then;
Fair Wyoming a heap of ashes laid;
The pitiless savage led by Christian men,
Our country claimed that retribution dire
Be tested till their bloody hands were stayed;
Yet wholesale slaughter such as Cromwell stained
Aroused in Washington but generous ire,
And while our settlements exposed remained,
The seaboard villages were swept by fire.
His noble heart indignantly constrained
Retaliate upon the treacherous foe
Repay such savage outrage blow for blow.
Not his to wage a war against the weak,
The helpless woman and the harmless child;
Yet well the country might resentment wreak
On hellish deed that Satan's self defiled.
From Erie's lake to where the Hudson flows
Its wealth of waters to our ocean mart,
From Wyoming, whose blackened embers glowed
With indignation in each generous heart,
To where the blue Ontario swells and heaves,
Niagara's tumultuous torrents foamed
Within a boundless wilderness of leaves,
Tribe upon tribe of dusky warriors roamed.
With many a trait their savage way retrieves;

Their grounds well tilled, commodious their abodes,
Their rights defined by laws both just and wise,
If not like ours their habits and their codes,
Champlain and Kirkland helped to civilize;
Trained to endure excruciating pain,
To inflict it on themselves and others too,
The frequent massacres their hands imbue,
Atrocities their bloody records stain,
The legends of their warlike race explain.
If from their sylvan solitudes concealed,
Science and art heaped up in ages flown
To their quick sense and faculties revealed
What their experience taught by nature shown.
Imaginative, astute, and eloquent,
In their confederate councils proud and grave,
Words rich in meaning stated what they meant,
And those that governed were both wise and brave.
Their chief pursuits the war-path and the chase,
Skilful in stratagem and the ambuscade,
By stars and trees and winds their foes they trace,
If oft deceived, occasionally betrayed,
Their prisoners tortured, burnt, or maimed, or flayed,
Not to retaliate, for savages, disgrace.
Where now so many Christian souls exist
In thriving cities, amidst teeming fields,
Scarce twoscore thousand Indians then subsist .

On fish or game the stream or forest yields,
On corn or garden growths, or orchards lent
Of luscious apples which the seasons sent.
Here the imperial realm of beauty spread
With graceful lakes in wooded mountains set,
Of wild ravines, with cataract, cascade;
Where Adirondack lifts its alp on alp,
Catskill looks eastward on the morning red,
In all this wilderness of sheen and shade,
The crafty huntsman for his quarry strayed
To kill his venison, or his foemen scalp.

On all the earth beneath its daily run
No fairer land illumined by the sun;
Here the five nations of the Iroquois,
Strong in their league, held other tribes at bay,
From when Champlain encountered them in war
Till Tuscaroras joined their proud array.
Where Mississippi rolls its turbid floods,
Beyond St. Lawrence which in ocean pours
The inland seas that bound us on the north,
Upon the war-path through the boundless woods
Their well-armed legions by skilled sachems led
From the longhouse Tioga issuing forth
Destroyed the Eries, Ottawas, Hurons drove,
Algonquins conquered, and the Illinois,

Leni Lenapes yielded to their sway,
The Shawanese Miamis vainly strove,
All in their turn this powerful league obey.

From Canada what they most valued came, —
Arms, ammunitions, waters strong;
Their chieftain's lovely sister bore the name
Of the king's regent, who had ruled them long,
Whose influence attached them to the crown;
And though his days on earth had reached their
    term,
That influence to his son descending down,
All but the Oneidas to the king stood firm.
They burn and massacre by English led,
They blocked our path to Fort Niagara,
And justified by wanton blood they shed,
The Congress ordered, and the troops obeyed.

When the French fleet expected on the shore,
The harvest ripe, too late for planting more,
Sullivan and Clinton with four thousand men
The country penetrate, its streams explore;
The loaded orchards' crops and dwellings burn
And drive their wily foes to Canada.
What Congress ordered Washington approved,
The few resisting slain, the weaker spared;

And for such arduous duty well prepared,
The army did its duty as behooved, —
In the projected expedition shared,
The season spent, back to their base return.

CANTO VII.

SAVANNAH.

CALM seas and fickle winds the French delay,
　　The tropic reached had many a spell to charm,
Its spicy odors, venom to betray,
The stanchest, of their vigor to disarm.
Scourged by disease, ships shattered by the gale,
The period wasted for the project planned,
Their Admiral, if true as told the tale,
Jealous of De Grasse he left in his command,
Perhaps to redeem his pledge, preserve his men
In healthier climes, on whom the scurvy preyed,
Or for himself some added glory gain,
The orders of his monarch disobeyed;
Home with his crippled ships forthwith return,
Informed Savannah undefended lay
Upon his homeward path and near at hand;
Vain-glorious hopes within his bosom burn,
Sanguine of victory he pursued his way,
His prows directed to the promised land.

Great the delight that thrilled along the shore,
With tidings that our allies come once more

With fleets and armies to our drooping hope;
Sumter and Marion, Laurens, Huger
Glow with the faith that we might yet be free,
With England's forty thousand veterans cope.
Lincoln at Charleston sends, by sail and oar,
Transports to bring the troops more near the place,
Fresh food and drugs from his own scanty store
The sick to cure, the slackened sinews brace;
The sister flags through land-locked Ossibaw
Speed through its shoals the gallant men of France,
Not many less than when, the year before,
The Newport breeze their kindred banners flaunt;
Weak and surprised, the place at once assailed
Been forced to yield, superior force prevailed.

From ships that rocked exposed, ten leagues away,
With sluggish toil they dragged their heavy guns;
Events beyond control their progress stay,
As midst the sands they work their weary way
Through bog and marsh, beneath the scorching suns;
And when at length the strengthened lines beset
The well-drilled ranks drawn up in proud array,
Summons to surrender crafty Prevost met.
Craving a truce but for a single day,
He would the terms proposed reflect upon;
But when his answer came, the time not yet,

Maitland had reinforced the garrison.
D'Estaing, untiring, his approaches made,
Lincoln from Charleston came with troops to aid;
Their progress Prescott warily delayed,
Obstructing streams and road, and bridges burnt;
Yet now, at last, the parallels were run,
From disappointment wise experience learnt,
Ceaseless the cannons roar, the dwellings blazed,
Horrors of which, mere apprehension crazed,
That Newport had so narrowly escaped;
Which Newport might quite possibly have won
Whose spectral forms mere apprehension shaped
The sturdier veterans cared not look upon.

Woman and child in vain for mercy prayed;
The Admiral some fiend with mockery dazed,—
It might be duty, or it might be pride,—
The prayed-for boon he, pitiless, denied.
If to this course humane objection pressed,
Doubtless his generous heart was sorely tried,
But his decision overruled the rest;
Woman and child in hapless frenzy died.
Meanwhile each day, near forty left aboard,
Released from suffering in their painless sleep,
The pale survivors, their own doom deplored,
Consigned with prayer the bodies to the deep.

Fifty huge guns belch forth their fateful fire,
Weak bearing shells explode in house and street,
Their track, though marked with rack and ruin
    dire,
Harmless against the strong defences beat.
Moncrief had girt the mound that Nature made,
Oglethorpe chosen for his citadel,
With demilune, redoubt, and palisade,
Could a whole host with slender guard repel.
With time and guns and forces adequate,
Gibraltar, Ehrenbreitstein, needs must fall;
The rules of science give their laws to fate,
And weak the hand that strikes against the wall.
D'Estaing imperious, restless, and disturbed,
With calmer judgment had attained his end,
But his impulsive temper raged uncurbed,
To wiser council all too proud to bend.
His king incensed, his rivals envious,
Disliked by officers, unloved by men,
Whatever course he took were perilous;
His cankered conscience could not guide him
    then.
The slaves to fate no more by reason led,
Grope feverish, blinded in the lurid gloom,
Shrink from the horrors they too justly dread,
And unresisting stagger to their doom.

The engineers with vigorous effort wrought,
Nor unmolested were the trenches flushed,
At night bold Graham sallied from the fort,
His puny force with no great effort crushed.
In larger numbers, well-concerted plan,
McArthur fought the pickets unprepared,
But as return the fire the French began,
The assailants to their lines in haste repaired.
When the report that only ten days more
Were needed to complete the parallels,
Batteries of the heaviest guns to pour
Directly on the forts their shot and shell,
D'Estaing, perverse, declares he cannot wait;
The rest decide, if so, to take their chance;
Great their disgrace if he should sail away,
Leave them again abandoned to their fate.
Better to storm before another dawn,
Attack the place with the whole force of France,
With near a thousand more by Lincoln led,
While Irish Dillon, though a Frenchman born,
Shall scale the work upon the river's bank;
Pulaski who in youth for Poland bled,
Now in his prime to give his life for us,
To strike the British on their western flank,
Happy in death to die for freedom thus.

Williams, Huger, with twice a thousand men
Make first a feigned attack upon the east,
Await the signal, and with ardor then
Assail the fortress where expected least.
Each on his breast to wear a badge of white,
To tell or friend or enemy at night;
Strange was the medley in that campans town,
French, British, Germans, Irish, and the Pole,
Americans fighting for, against the crown
Hessians in chains to trample freedom down;
Brave men for freedom from unjust control,
Fathers and sons opposed, embattled stood;
Brothers for pottage shed each other's blood
A traitor in the camp for gold revealed
The plan of combat to the proud Prevost,
Who at the menaced points, his strength concealed,
To parry the attack give blow for blow.
The march delayed, it was already dawn
When D'Estaing, Lincoln, moved to the attack;
But from the first it was a hope forlorn,
And streams of blood their onward footsteps track,
As all along their ranks their comrades fell,
And dying heaps their instant danger tell.

The deadly cannon, from their view concealed,
Swept with results their withering ranks revealed;

Too stanch to yield, no panic drives them back.
Lincoln, with brave Laurens and McIntosh,
First rend the lines and enter the redoubt;
Those that defend yield to the onward rush
While serried masses press without.
The grape and shrapnel find an easy mark.
They seek in vain for covert here and there;
The shielded corners promised in the dark
Proved in the daylight but a fatal snare.
Bush, Holmes, the rampart scale, their colors plant
  Beside the French; Gray, fearless, shakes them
      free.
The bullets slay whom danger cannot daunt,
For the third time bold Jasper raised the flag,
Four heroes fell and died for liberty.
For a long hour a close and withering fire
Plays on the masses all along the trench,
And hundreds weltering in their gore lay dead;
Americans lost as many as the French.
They still fought on, trusting in those that led;
But all in vain their guns the ramparts rent,
Efforts to scale and storm, disaster met.
Pulaski slain, and wounded twice D'Estaing,
He with his troops retreated to his ships;
Such disappointment he could not forget,
Though to repining, pride might seal his lips.

He long lived on, a broken-hearted man,
Till on the scaffold ended his regret.

Thus menaced by his foes in field and siege,
Who, far apart, wrought better than they knew,
Beyond the lakes Canadians still liege;
The Carolina tories stanch and true,
To hold them loyal, steadfast to the Crown,
Needed for their protection armaments
Their monarch, sore beset, but ill could spare.
Nor bravely struggling in their own defence
With slight success and even less renown,
In costly warfare against France and Spain,
Would his home subjects heavier burthens bear;
Nor might he hope his previous gems retain
If fleets and armies battered down their walls.
The terrors of the summers past renew,
As on the dim horizon's farthest verge
The ships of France fade sadly from the view;
The Admiral o'er his withered laurels broods
And all life has of bitterness recalls,
As Sullivan, Clinton, in fresh strength emerge
From the autumnal splendor of the woods.
Their country's gain rich realms of pasture new;.
England from Newport hauls her colors down,
Off from the isle her iron clutch withdrew.

As thus the evil genius of the war
Upon the surges of the ocean tost,
Whose haste had drenched Savannah's sands in gore,
The maimed and halt regained their ranks no more,
Lincoln was crippled, and Pulaski lost.

December, 1779.

As closed the year, from Newport now set free,
Seven thousand veterans to Charleston sent,
With the victorious legions Prevost lent,
With guns afloat the land defences rent,
And Clinton gained an easy victory.
Congress commands the conqueror of Burgoyne
The progress of the enemy to stay;
Sumter, De Kalb, his feeble armies join.
Gates scorned advice, his pride his steps betray;
He marched at night, mischance his troops delay,
Confronts Cornwallis, who with equal force
Wonted to battle, strong in discipline,
In Webster, Rawdon, Hamilton, McLeod,
In bayonets, artillery, and horse, —
What chance, against such odds, had Gates to win?
For wise retreat to safer grounds, too proud;
Two-thirds his army, boastful pledge forgot,
Before their assailants fled without a shot.
In vain the regulars, of sterner mould,

From Maryland and doughty Delaware,
Throughout the conflict boldest of the bold,
Did all at Camden stoutest man could dare.

August 16, 1780.

They bravely fought, and held their foe at bay,
Lost heavily, and yet refused to yield;
Strong in their closed up ranks, without dismay
They, the last remnant left upon the field, —
All others fled, De Kalb their general slain,
Vanished from view, till gathering in their strength,
Convinced not theirs the battle to retrieve,
One-half their number joined their chief at length.
Gates, forced along by the retreating crowd,
Two hundred miles with one companion rode.
Gloomy the thoughts his saddened spirit shroud,
What such disaster for the cause forbode;
Perhaps, too, mourned that his once brilliant fame,
Brave men at Saratoga helped to earn,
Tarnished and blurred in Camden's day of shame,
Had lost its lustre never to return.

As Newport's roses in its gardens bloom,
Maidens demure in gala thronged its streets,
Far in the offing heard the welcome boom;
And thirty ships of France, now come to stay,

Stalk in their pride the waters of the bay.
Each fort along the shore their advent greets;
Their admiral, the admirable Ternay,
Soon sleeps in death upon this foreign shore.
The British fleet for months soon blocks the way,
Before, in force sufficient to withdraw,
There too remain at least four thousand men,
Commanded by the gentlemen of France, —
The princely Rochambeau and Chattallux,
Henry, Deux-ponts, Vioménil, Leuzun;
With all the virtues noble blood enhance,
In the esteem of all they daily grew.
And though their sojourn ending all too soon,
Tradition still can tell what happened there, —
The festal banquet and the graceful dance;
Homage polite that pleases yet not harms;
The gracious intercourse of word and glance
That lends to French society its charms,
And wins for all affection everywhere.

Not strange each breast with grateful feeling glows
Towards protectors from unnatural foes,
Whose Hess and Indian bloodhounds sack, maraud,
No limit to their insatiate greed content,
Their kinsfolk of their honest rights defraud,
While unsubdued remains the continent.

For sordid trade, or vanity more drear,
Covet the earth, their knees in suppliance bent,
Nor heed the hate, can they inspire the fear;
Guns for their reason, for their sceptre, sword,
Can brutal deed but further their intent;
The deeds of savage, white or red, applaud,
Taught to believe what for advantage tells,
Duping the ignorant by wiles and spells
That oligarchs may rule at home, abroad.
Well may the Quaker maids their joy express,
Their tyrants now too distant to oppress.

For conquests now their foes seek genial field
Where scanty bands by Sumter, Marion, led
By sturdy blows the royalists repress;
If oft defeated, know not how to yield;
Even when defeated still help on the cause;
By generalship and daring win applause.
If of one mind, for freedom or for Crown,
The Carolinas had been doubly strong,
The last faint spark of freedom trampled down,
Or driven out the myrmidons of wrong.
A house divided 'gainst itself must fall;
Brothers and kin in hostile ranks arrayed,
Revenge its bitterest enmities displayed,
And party rage the nearest friends betrayed,

Prompted to arts the vilest soul appall.
Thus blind, perverse, their enemies pursue
Their wonted course to triumph o'er the weak,
Breeding dissensions, those resist subdue,
Who, in despair, the king's protection seek.

October 16, 1780.

Tarleton below Broad River kills and burns;
Above its waters Ferguson marauds,
Watching for Clarke, who from a raid returns, —
Rest for his troops, King's Mountain, near, affords.
Shelby, McDonnel, Campbell, Seviers,
All colonels, rouse to arms the country-side;
Moss-troopers bold, whose well-trained officers
For pass or ford can need no surer guide.
In numbers equal sixteen hundred men,
The rebels scale the hill, and, driven back,
With greater vigor storm its heights again.
When Ferguson killed, his men their efforts slack,
Discouraged by the south they strive in vain.
For one whole hour the desperate fight proceeds,
Three thousand men with mutual slaughter rife
De Peyster, who to Ferguson succeeds,
Pulls down his colors, and thus ends the strife.
Some doubtless fled, concealed in wood or glen;
That battle cost the king a thousand men.

November 3, 1780.

At Blackstock, wounded, Sumter held the ground;
Each side a hundred lost, yet would not yield.
The turbid streams of Yadken and of Dan
With blood of whigs and tories freely ran;
But neither claimed the honor of the field.
From far Niagara, with his savage bands
Johnson swooped down upon the Mohawk vale,
Drove out the Oneidas from their homes and lands,
But widespread havoc left to tell the tale.

Arnold, in debt, despairing of the cause,
Which well seemed hopeless when D'Estaing went
    home,
For rank and gold, all heedless of the laws
Of honor, or the shame that needs must come
To his descendants, sold himself away;
Nor himself only, promised to betray
Our strongholds to the foe; and while André,
As his accomplice, on the scaffold died,
He fled from wrath, and mourned for many a day
He had not also perished by his side.

What knee but bends, what bosom but must glow
With homage to the patriotic men
From whose example our best blessings flow! —

For freedom gained an easy victory then.
No nobler characters on historic page
Than theirs in Congress shaped our destiny;
Their glory handed down from age to age
Till the fast fetters rust, of slavery.
No one more honored than the loved Laurens,
When D'Estaing first arrived, its president
To foreign courts to multiply our friends,
Its best of suppliants by Congress sent,
Captured at sea, committed to the tower,
The fate of André tempted to requite,
His old associates did what in their power
To extricate him from his hapless plight.

After six years of service in the camp
And in the Congress, Sullivan again
With zeal and faith, no hopes discouraged, damp,
Still boldly advocates the rights of men.
His long experience in the arts of war,
Knowledge complete of what the army needs,
Of government, the mysteries of law,
His faithful services, and well-known deeds
Gave him an influence, with few to share
The many duties that the times devolve.
Wise to decide, and ever bold to dare,
Quick to devise, and prudently resolve,

No one more ably could its problems solve.
Settling with Madison the claims of Spain,
Establishing credit and the needed bank,
Arranging controversies of pay and rank,
Reorganizing armies, sending Greene
To do what Gates endeavored to in vain,
In his sole charge instructions to Laurens,
Sent out to France to liberate his sire,
Whom when at Newport he had known so well,
He moved and wrote a letter to the king
For John to carry, and perhaps inspire
With sense of what the coming year might bring:
The war protracted to a happy end,
If the allies united efforts lend.

John, like his sire, generous and brave,
With every trait and grace ennobles man,
Who, at Savannah charging in the van,
Wounded, had just escaped a soldier's grave,
With Franklin, — heaven its own artillery gave, —
Vergennes, and the king matured the plan
Destined, in time, our cause imperilled save.

As chill December brought its earliest frost,
Greene superseding Gates in his command,
They meet and part in friendly courtesy.

Both knew too well how battles may be lost,
Not what their own, but what their country's cost;
Not, in all kindness to be frank and free,
Less than a thousand men with Gates remained;
These were enhungered, and their garments stained.
But Morgan came, and, ordered to the west,
Guarded the rivers to their mountain source,
While Marion, in simple homespun dressed,
Watched all the streams along their ocean course.
Greene's kinsman bold came too, four hundred strong,
Who raised for Butt's Hill the freedman's corps,
Whose doughty deeds to every age belong,
Soon to be victim of a shameless wrong;
To slay who yields, a crime by knighthood's law.
Washington and Lee had brought as many more;
Greene with them all had twice a thousand told.
Leslie, almost as strong, from Charleston sped
To reinforce the British chiefs, who hold
Winnsboro, seventy miles away, ill clothed and fed.
Cornwallis orders Tarleton intercept
Morgan, who guards the rapid Pacolet;
With work to do Tarleton but lightly slept.

January 11, 1781.

At dawn he marched, at nine at Cowpens met
Morgan's eight hundred Marylanders bold;

Virginians, Georgians, formed upon the crest;
Four hundred, lower down, their fire withhold
Till their assailants meet them breast to breast.
When Pickens orders, they pour in their ball,
Then, veiled in smoke, they disappear from sight
Behind the hill, on Washington, McCall,
To ground beyond well sheltered by a wood;
But proved the need to reinforce the right,
Tarleton pressed on, ascends the sloping ground
With his dragoons, foot, and artillery.
Fierce their assault, and as our right swung round
For Pickens' horse to flank, misunderstood,
Ordered when hardly pressed to shift their ground,
The force turned round to retrograde or flee;
When Morgan, vexed, too cool to be disturbed,
In tones resistless their impatience curbed,
Ordered a halt; to right about and rush
With bayonets fixed, upon the foe surprised.

January 7, 1781.

McCall and Washington their right flank crush;
And their whole army, now demoralized,
Yield to the victors they so late despised.
Tarleton met Washington in the mêlée,
His own hand cut, shoots Washington in the knee,
With forty of his troopers rides away,

Leaving to Morgan a great victory.
Another thousand of our foes the less,
Who for their king their fellow-men oppress.

Cornwallis, in dire need of clothes and food,
His army now reduced to half its strength,
Assured that farther north the tories stood
In readiness to help him if they might,
Crossing the Dan he ventures on at length;
Leslie with succor follows in his rear,
Delayed by streams to pass and roads to clear;
Greene diligently strove to stay their course
Until his army ready for the prey,
Then calling in his infantry and horse
With such recruits as he could find at hand,
Long held his skilled antagonist at bay.
Part of his troops could not much longer stay,
And his own force as large as that opposed.

At Guilford Court House, resolved to make a stand,
For each event might chance his battle planned,
His trustiest men and those less skilled disposed.
Butler and Easton to command the front,
Singleton's guns within the centre placed;
Those least reliable by veterans braced,

Since upon them devolved to bear the brunt.
Lynch with his rifles, Washington with his horse,
Kirkwood's brave Delawares to flank the right,
While Campbell's rifles, Legion under Lee,
That Light-horse Harry, famed in many a fight,
Shield in the forest dense the other wing.
Stanch, strong enough, would seem that stalwart
    force
Even sturdy Britons to a stand to bring.
Three hundred yards behind, Virginia's sons,
The sons of freedom, chiefly volunteer,
Good marksmen all and wonted to their guns,
On either side the outskirts of the wood,
To harass, destroy all within range, appear,
In case the front should not the foe withstand.
Higher up the hill, about as far beyond,
The regulars with officers well skilled, —
One-half Virginians, brave Huger's command,
The rest from Maryland by Williams drilled.

May 15, 1781.

The art of war few better understand,
Not many in the battle-field before;
Hands often tremble first shed human blood.
Could our own death in battle but discharge
Our duty, better sleep forevermore

Than soar aloft with others' blood imbrued;
But custom states to every thought like this,
Good soldiers fear not death, nor shrink to kill.
Perhaps for Greene the glory of the day,
If from his lines no ball had gone amiss,
So well was fought the battle on the hill.

The British ranks, of tougher metal made,
Their work in life to combat and destroy;
Leslie, who brings three regiments in aid,
Commands the right, and bids his troops deploy.
The Seventy-first fights, Hessians in the front,
One-half the Guards with Norton in support.
Webster that bloody day, as was his wont,
Brave of the bravest ever in the front,
From mortal wounds to be of life bereft,
His own and Thirty-fourth compose the left,
With Grenadiers and Second Guards in rear.
Light Infantry and Jagers guard the guns,
While Tarleton farther back no danger shuns,
Keeps to the road, impatient bides his chance
To charge like knight of old with sword and lance;
Wherever needed, like a flash appear.

McLeod's artillery twenty minutes played.
The Carolinians firmly kept their ranks;

But when the British charged as on parade,
The militia broke, sought shelter on the flanks.
Part in their panic reached the second line,
Which, joined by Kirkwood, Lynch, and Washing-
    ton,
Closed bravely up, confront the advancing foe,
Who with fixed bayonets still came speeding on.
Reserves brought up in line as on they go,
As Campbell's rifles, Legion under Lee,
Harass their right as steady on they sweep.
Rose and O'Hara towards the forest wheel;
But from its thickets' dusky coverts steep
The deadly sting from hidden rifles feel,
Cannot resent on foes not theirs to see.
The rest press on. Long the Virginians hold
Their ground with spirit, but at last give way
On Continentals, rally those most bold,
Yet not enough to save the losing day.

The ground was rough, the woods and thickets
    dense;
Deep, dark ravines impede their upward course.
Their ranks disordered by rock, brook, and fence,
Thinned by the rifles, harried by the horse,
Their front diminished to protect their flanks,

These lusty bull-dogs ravined for their prey.
The Grenadiers and Guards O'Hara led,
With Webster's own battalion, reach the fray,
Charge on the regulars, whose steady fire
Staggers their rush and smites their withering ranks;
Gunsley with bayonets drives the Thirty-third
Down the steep slopes, across the wooded glen.
Up the rough hillside pant the scattered herd,
Till Webster finds some covert for his men.
Well might Greene think for us the battle won,
So well that day had Maryland dared and done.

Meanwhile, O'Hara's Guards and Grenadiers
Charged to the left the Second Maryland,
Composed in part of recent volunteers,
Who near the Court House on the left wing stand.
Soon overwhelmed in combat hand to hand,
The guns committed to their charge were lost;
The Guards, unseen, had almost reached their rear,

Crowding the Americans, when Webster near,
His men refreshed, the ravine recrossed,
Stood firm till other regiments appear
Which resistance down below belates,

As he, impatient for their coming, waits.
The Maryland First before had driven him back,
Of braver temper, warming with their task,
Wheeled left, and with their bayonets attack,
Repulse, and slay' foes that no quarter ask;
While Washington's horsemen trampled down and
    slew
All that still dared to keep the open ground.
Stewart, their colonel, and many scores
Of his best soldiers bleeding lay around;
The guns, retaken, posted on a knoll,
Had stopped Cornwallis, and the battle won.
Yet in the medley, who could all control?
By slight mischance the Americans undone.

Long Campbell's rifles, Legion under Lee,
Had fought the Hessians and the Seventy-first,
Shooting them down from every rock and tree, —
Those that resisted suffering the most.
Cornwallis, hearing this incessant fire,
Sent Tarleton in their strait to lend them aid,
As Lee, not knowing the destruction dire
His well-aimed balls of his opponents made,
Clearing away all obstacles between,
Speeded his forces on to strengthen Greene.
Thus freed, the Twenty-third and Seventy-first,

Tarleton's dragoons, Cornwallis with his guns,
From woods below into the open burst,
While Webster strikes, his former foes reversed.
Not even then brave Greene the combat shuns.
He still fought on, till two full hours had flown
Since first this well contested strife began;
And had the weakness of his foe been known,
Success had sealed the wisdom of his plan.
To useless bloodshed his kind breast averse,
Prudence persuaded him to spare his troops,
Whose hope of triumph, not whose courage droops.
His cousin Cristopher covered his retreat
To rendezvous assigned, where all should meet;
Morgan predicted, should the militia fight,
Greene would come off the conqueror that day;
If, as it happened, they should take to flight,
Be cut to pieces; but they marched away.

Our dwindling ranks, unpaid, unclad, unfed,
Resources wasting, and no credit left;
Children and wives a-clamor for their bread,
Our shams for gold, of all their work bereft;
Allies at Newport under strict blockade;
The timid wavering, armies mutinied,
Traitors for pelf our fortresses betrayed;
But slight the hope our country would be freed,

While thus the lukewarm freedom's cause desert.
Henry Laurens, a prisoner in the tower,
Congress, the doom that menaced to avert,
Besought King Louis to exert his power,
Deputing John Laurens, wise, generous, brave,
With every gift and trait ennoble man,
Who late had but escaped a soldier's grave,
Hit at Savannah, charging in the van,
To make the friendly king direct appeal
For men and means, and to adjust a plan
To such conditions as events reveal.
Franklin, Vergennes, when heard his purpose bold,
Doubts of its prudence could but ill conceal;
Still in fit phrase the youth his story told,
Placing in royal hand the missive sent.
His gallant mien fresh force the suppliance lent;
And as with courtly grace his knee he bent,
His doughty deeds his ather's perils plead.
Called by the monarch round his council board,
The various obstacles and chances scanned,
Before the winter gone, with one accord
These noblemen the coming campaign planned;
Louis, whose millions generously bestowed
For our enfranchisement cost him life and crown,
Laurens, whose breast with patriot fervor glowed,
Franklin, from heaven drew the lightning down,

Vergennes, sagacious, who could not forget
The widespread realms Albion had wrenched from
    France,
Decide how best Cornwallis be beset,
Ensnared, and captured, with prophetic glance.
What they conclude, in secret cipher sent,
With the May blossoms camp and Congress reach;
And Louis wrote how, by reverses bent,
England had sued for terms reverses teach.
He urged the Congress every effort make
That they might with the more advantage treat,
Promising France would every measure take
For independence, guard against defeat.
He promised gold and ships and rich supplies
To pay and arm our soldiers in the field;
From southern seas De Grasse the foe surprise
With ample troops to force Cornwallis yield.

CAMDEN, *April* 5, 1781.

While the victorious Earl, in bitter grief,
One-fourth his army slain, or wounded, lay,
Reposed his stricken host for respite brief,
Then by slow marches plodded on his way
In search of Phillips, sent to his relief,
His active rival south to Camden sped
To strike at Rawdon, block his progress north,

Impede his march to Charleston if he fled,
Should fortune favor, draw his army forth,
Cripple, if not subdue, the force he led.
To effect these objects, Marion sent out,
Captured Fort Watson with his crib of sand,
Seized on the passes all along the route,
Cut Watson off, who, quitting his redoubt,
Led reinforcements to his chief's command.
Rawdon's own army, but a thousand strong,
Were well compacted, vigorous and bold;
His dauntless spirit which no odds appall,
He gains the forest, pounces on the fold.
His onslaught, Morgan, Benson, Kirkwood, held at bay,
While Greene with promptness marshalled his array,
Huger his right, Williams the left with Ford;
Guns placed between the surer havoc make
On triple ranks than musketry or sword.

The foe consists of Campbell's Sixty-third,
In Newport's by-ways met such heavy loss;
Americans who foreign yoke preferred
To sharing with their country freedom's cross;
Behind them marched the Irish volunteers
To bind us to the thraldom, ground their own;

Then Carolinians with their hopes and fears;
Dragoons, to whom such weakness all unknown.

Rawdon, in order to extend his van,
Called up his troops in rear to both his flanks;
Greene takes advantage of this change of plan
To charge upon them while confused their ranks.
This led to some disorder in his lines;
And many fell, both officers and men.
Before he could reorganize again,
The able Campbell his best course divines,
Sweeps up the hill with his well ordered force,
Pierces the weakened centre, takes the guns,
And gains the crest with infantry and horse.
Greene quickly sees all farther effort vain
Recover ground thus lost; the slaughter ends.
Washington sent to strike the foe in rear,
At Logtown posted, covers the retreat;
If the pursuers follow up too near,
His fearless charges their attempts defeat.
Both sides lost heavily—each one-fourth its men—
Before the combatants their camps regain.

Arnold, the venal, as the year began,
With sixteen hundred Scotch and loyalists
Raided Virginia, Richmond sacked and burned,

And had not Jefferson thwarted all his plans,
Experienced Steuben forced him to desist,
Had carried off the spoils ignobly earned.
Lafayette, despatched by Washington,
With force too scant to conquer in the field,
Prevented yet what greater mischief done.
Arnold, with no solace for his sore,
Which neither British rank nor money healed,
Disgrace no stronghold strong enough to shield
The penalty, like that which Judas bore,
Tidings in May of Phillips close at hand
With ample succor to Cornwallis, cheers;
But Phillips dying, Arnold took command,
And for ten days, until the Earl appear,
Has under him, near by, four thousand men.
His brief authority surrendered then,
He hastened north to raid his native State,
Thus forfeiting all pity for his fate.

Muhlenberg, Steuben, Lafayette, and Wayne —
Illustrious names nor time nor envy blur —
From British rule the Old Dominion wrenched,
Rallying the farmers with fit words that stir.
With force inferior, oft advantage gain,
And if the land with little bloodshed drenched,
Arnold and Phillips easily repressed

By march and counter-march and false alarm,
Tarleton, alert, in peril never sleeps;
Baffled, perplexed, pursuing phantoms vain,
His bold dragoons over the country sweeps,
Though all his efforts powerless to harm.
Even Cornwallis, ever wise and calm,
At last disheartened, thoughtful of his men,
Weary and worn, by scorching heats oppressed,
Yorktown and Gloucester chosen for their rest,
With deep forebodings lest no succor come
From Clinton, or expected ships from home,
He bides what time may bring with anxious breast.

Eutaw Springs, *September* 8, 1781.

In tropic heats, in desultory war,
Sumter and Marion, Horry, Hampton, Lee,
Close up the gates of Charleston near and far,
The region round about from thraldom free.
Greene, on the Sand Hills in supreme command,
Watched for his chance to inflict some telling blow.
The sea breeze fanned to health his little band.
Friends kept advised of what behooved to know.
When crops were harvested, his force grew strong,
Pickens and Marion, summoned, came in aid.
He knew that Stewart, after waiting long
At Orange for supplies, mishap delayed,

As his famished army ill could spare
Sufficient detail guard against maraud,
Moved on himself to meet them, lest some snare
Should block their progress with such foes abroad.
Learning that Greene approached with this intent,
He drew his army back to Eutaw Springs,
Scouts to observe the hostile movements sent,
Chosen his ground, and bides what fortune brings;
Resolved not to attack, but to resist,
Majoribanks posts in thickets on his right,
The Irish Buffs and Cruger's royalists,
The Sixty-third and fourth and Coffin's horse.
Two thousand men stood ready for the fight,
Should their assailants bring superior force.
An ancient mansion served them for a fort,
Its garden fenced by lofty palisade;
To render this impregnable they sought,
Should aught disastrous need such sheltering aid.

Greene's force from lack of discipline was weak;
In guns and muskets it was weaker yet.
And soldiers, sorely pressed, will safety seek,
Who never in the field have foemen met.
Pickens and Marion command his wings;
Between, were levies from the State at large;
Behind, three small brigades of higher rank

Sumner and Campbell, Williams, have in charge.
Washington, Kirkwood, with reserve in rear,
And Lee and Henderson on either flank,
Deployed in line, as they came marching near.
In the advance a pioneer descried
Some seven-score men on foraging intent, —
These and the foragers Greene's lawful prize,
As also forty troopers scouting sent.

At nine, the armies for the fray opposed,
The artillery its booming thunders sounds;
The British troops of their best men composed.
Greene's line, unflinching, bold beyond its wont,
Fired on their opponents some twenty rounds,
Who not for that their vigorous efforts slack;
When Greene's weak centre in the pressure break,
Reserves with promptitude position take,
With bayonets drive the British left wing back.
Scattered, disheartened, they safe shelter find
In the brick mansion strongly fortified,
While Stewart his disordered ranks aligned,
Withdrawn to grounds that lay his camps behind,
Enhungered farmers to their danger blind
Plunder and revel with a wolfish pride.
His men were by success demoralized,
By such unseemly conduct vexed, surprised;

And Washington, captured by Majoribanks in the
    wood,
Seeing his soldiers slaughtered where they stood,
Greene gathered up his troops as best he could,
And led them back till far enough beyond
The turmoil of such stricken battle-field.

If that day's work no signal triumph yield,
The loss inflicted was twice that sustained.
To Greene's great soul, to his established fame
Mattered but little battles lost or gained;
The work he had to do was ably done.
A few weeks later, when his force regained
The post upon the Sand Hills, his to know
Cornwallis and the fleet had been constrained
To yield to Washington and Rochambeau.
Charleston a British garrison remained
For months too strong to take, nor cause for blame;
Not his to waste a life by needless blow.

CANTO VIII.

SURRENDER.

LIVES there the man unwilling to admit
    The hand of Providence in every hour;
Who doth not to its sovereign will commit
Our human life to His superior power?
If all the stars that in their orbits roll,
By Him created, in His guiding care
Speed on their way, in His divine control,
Why should not nations in its mercy share?
If so designed, why not co-operate?
To effect its purposes, events seem strange.
We cannot tell what influences work,
What gracious motives may in secret lurk,
The future destiny of our race to change.
Issues of battle much on chance depend;
The course of campaign's oft involved in doubt.
The fickle winds and various causes send
Defeat or triumph, not for us find out;
Inscrutable to us, should His love ordain
What in its wisdom is for us the best,

For races, nations, whether loss or gain.
How can we question the divine behest
Allured Cornwallis to the fatal trap,
The fetters of colonial bondage snap?

In blustering March, the king in council sate;
And by his side Vergennes, Franklin, Laurens,
How best to end the war deliberate
With pondering brows and ever thoughtful pens.
Laurens, sore crippled in Savannah's fight,
Wearing his shattered arm still in his sling, —
Of French descent, his sires Huguenot,
A gallant soldier, without blemish, blot, —
With D'Estaing fought for their country's right,
Won the affection of the generous king.
With growing pride in their assured success,
No thoughts of prudence wise Vergennes depress;
Encouraged by tidings recent letters bring,
Their sanguine expectations all express.
The French at Newport with their strengthened
    fleet,
Clinton's appeals for instant aid from home;
Perplexed how compass Cornwallis' retreat,
Protect his scattered armies from defeat,
Impatient waits for what events may come,
Eager to purchase sure intelligence.

His shrewd antagonists baffle all his schemes,
And much more honest, have sufficient sense
To set at nought all his ambitious dreams.

As the May-flowers denote the coming spring,
To Congress brought the answer of the king,
His promised millions and concerted plan;
De Grasse to come with every ship and man
From southern seas; and when occasion rife,
Moment auspicious to conclude the strife,
The enemy make overtures for peace, —
Russia and Austria had of late proposed,
If so desired, terms to arbitrate.
Should, at that time, Americans be strong
When the agreements for the peace be closed,
Claim all the continent to them belong,
To keep their independence as a State,
He earnestly besought them not forego
Any exertions that will help their cause,
And should the chances come to strike the blow,
Be sure to conquer with the world's applause.
The thirty members, then, were all composed
The government of our extended realm,
Greeted the royal missive with acclaim;
Their grateful hearts with warmest fervor glow
To Louis, from whose grace such blessings flow.

On the committee raised to end the war
Served Sullivan, at Newport in command,
Who in December moved to make the appeal
To the French king to aid us in our strait;
As sole committee sent Laurens to France,
Prompted by Providence and not by fate.
No pains were spared to carry out behests
So kindly counselled by the gracious king,
To make the preparations he requests,
The dire confusion into order bring.
The fam'd Ithuriel with his magic spear
Revived our credit, filled each shrunk brigade;
And long before the fleets of France appear,
We ready stood in all our strength arrayed

We left Cornwallis hemmed around by foes,
By seas environed, pent up hard and fast;
His eager eyes scanned wearily the capes
With hope some friendly fleet appear at last.
His sorry plight went whispering on the breeze;
It reached Washington and Rochambeau,
Who, near the Hudson, from amidst the trees
Watch for a chance to make New York their own.
Or, should De Grasse, as then expected, come
With his strong fleet, be hovering on the coast,
Or any British squadron sent from home,

On the alert, no precious moment lost.
Now quick to know the longed-for fleet was near,
Their change of purpose in their camp unknown,
Pretending there they meant to strike the blow,
Around its works they wend their way with care,
And ere the foes suspect had melted in the air,
Speeding away three hundred miles below,
To where the Earl remained in anxious doubt.
No time was wasted; soon beleaguering stood
Full sixteen thousand men around the place,
With half that number in the garrison.
From out the bay De Grasse all cruisers chase
In partial combats; the victory won,
Approaches led against the British lines,
Dismount their guns, and burrow through their mines.
The works protecting, little blood was shed.
In reconnoitring, noble Scammell fell, —
Sullivan's loved pupil, both in law and war.
His wound was mortal, and he fought no more;
His deeds immortal, generations tell.
When all prepared to storm the bastions
That block the way with well-directed guns,
To capture one, to Lafayette assigned
With Laurens and Gimet and Hamilton;
Another to VioméniI, Deux-ponts.

Both parties scaled the ramparts as designed.
Gimet fell lifeless, entering the fort;
Barber, who led the American support,
The cannon spiked, reduced the garrison.

The Grenadiers in Rochambeau's command
In times remote had earned themselves the name,
" Auvergne sans tache," by some misfortune lost.
He promised them if they retrieved their fame
By doing well that night, he would demand
Of their good king their name should be restored;
They did their duty at but little cost,
King Louis did not wait to be implored.
His guns all silenced, and no succor near,
By wounds or capture lost five hundred men,
Life to his officers and soldiers dear,
Cornwallis knows to struggle longer vain;
To fly or yield, alternatives remain.
The council summoned, for their flight prepared
To seek the south at night, the waters cross.
Part wend their way, but soon the lightnings glare,
Rain in torrents fell, waves on waves in tempest
    toss.
On waves so troubled, but poorly fare
The crowded boats when they the passage dare;
Their flight thus hopeless, laws of war compel

Accept the terms prescribed the year before
To the Americans when Charleston fell.

The terms at Charleston, harsher far than now,
Cornwallis' cheek with the remembrance burns;
The poisoned chalice to the lip that sent,
A bitter yet a wholesome draught returns.
Adversity his haughty spirit bent;
Saddened and sore he cared not to appear,
Pleading indisposition for excuse.
He bids O'Hara render up his sword,
Which Washington and Rochambeau refuse,
Pointing to Lincoln, who, in saddle near,
Received with courtesy, and then restored.
Eight thousand prisoners with ship and gun
Fall to the victors, and thus ends the war.
For though eight years elapsed since Lexington,
Before the treaty signed that brought us peace,
With freedom, independence from the yoke,
That glorious day colonial fetters broke.
If in Laurens war claimed one victim more,
The clash of arms, fraternal slaughters cease;
A nation battle-born to life awoke,
And raised in peace its banner to the breeze.

CENTENNIAL.

OUR blood-bought freedom tested by the strain
    Of five-score years of weakness and of strife,
When party rage had spent its force in vain,
A war of sections but renewed its life;
Our people, taught what freedom signified,
Paid grateful homage to illustrious sires,
Renounced allegiance to a despot prince,
Ventured what held most dear, for country died,
With the fierce ardor liberty inspires
Regained their rights, our precious heirloom since.

For eight long years continued jubilee,
As each centennial builds its sacred shrine,
For priceless privilege of being free,
Their votive offerings, not of corn or wine,
But hearts devout to that great Source divine
Whence comes what renders life a boon to be.
We visited the halls where freedom born,
Rocked in its cradle, reared to manhood's strength
In many tribulations, oft forlorn,
Drove out the tyrant myrmidons at length.

Its battles we fought over, lost or won,
Not the less glorious, ending in defeat,
Sure no disgrace, for they their best had done,
Ever victorious when they equals meet;
Neither despondent when reverses came,
Nor yet elate, though triumph gild their name.
The glorious aim for which they strike the blow,
Mankind set free, through all the ages' flow.

When Rhoda's turn, one-half the epoch passed,
Her well-fought battle to commemorate,
To her chief city flocked a concourse vast
Of hearts aglow from every neighboring State,
With men renowned from recent battle-field,
Or won their spurs in the pursuits of peace.
The bar and bench and senate-chamber yield
Their best and noblest; historic men increase
The brilliant throng, and they that history write.
How many since that day by their decease
By deed or word have left their record bright!
Arnold and Allen, Damon ever dear,
Burnside, at Petersburg who led the charge,
Beloved by all, have closed their earth's career,
Who then, untrembling, stood upon its marge.

With one who bore his honored grandsire's name,
Commander in the fight, the century gone,

We joined the group of men well-known to fame,
Welcomed by those who well their work had done.
With all the pomp and pageantry of war,
With festal cannon and with martial air,
The long parade its floating banners bore
'Neath floral arches and 'mid maidens fair;
Down the broad stream the thronged vessels glide,
Their pennons streaming in the vernal sun,
While merry thousands lining either side
Greet their approach with jocund cheer or gun.

We disembarked upon Aquidneck's strand,
From Bristol Ferry marched to Butts's crest,
And gathering round its mouldering ramparts, scanned
The spreading waters and that narrow land
So long ago by hostile thousands pressed.
The woods had gone, and shrunken brooks were dry;
The clustering hills stood fast, once stained by gore;
Few were the habitations met the eye,
And Anthony's no mark of battle bore.
Some aged neighbors designate each spot
Where all the changes of the fight were fought;
Yet how much more, throughout all time forgot,

Tradition might have told, in season sought.
Not far from where that vigorous bayonet charge
Drove back the routed foemen from the ground,
Stretched banquet hall beneath whose canvas large
File in the illustrious throng, as loud resound
A salvo of artillery to the day;
The first, perhaps, that woke the echoes round
Since the hill shook beneath their hungry roar,
Since that dark night, a hundred years before,
Sullivan with his army crossed the bay.

As the last echo slowly died away,
The chaplain, fittingly, his task performs;
Arnold, the State's historian, eloquent,
In glowing words recalls the faded forms,
The din of battle, and the desperate strife.
And as his stirring periods filled the tent,
The long-passed scene came thrillingly to life.
Embattled armies on the hills opposed,
The serried masses, as the foes descend,
Their fierce encounter as in combat closed;
Guns shake the earth, the azure welkin rend,
Their missiles, hurtling, through battalions tore;
Incessant musketry too near to err,
Wounded and dead that to the 'rear they bore.
The charge retreat, the volley, and the stir

Of near ten thousand in that pent-up vale;
Unflinching, fearless, prodigal of blood,
Each breast all eager that his side prevail,
The long-drawn lines that patient, steadfast stood,
No lip that quivered, and no cheek that blenched
As venal Hessian, and the freedmen true,
Briton, who would our liberties have wrenched,
And all the world to his harsh rule subdue;
Patriots, resolved no more in suppliance sue
To haughty king, or bear his hated yoke,
Upon that field of carnage wrapt in smoke,
Lay down to life's last sleep, content to know
Who would be free, themselves must strike the blow.
And as the orator in clarion tones
From Proctor's verse Ravenna's fight rehearsed, —
The shout of triumph and the dying groans
As Wellington Napoleon's host dispersed, —
Each glistening eye, each swelling breast, reveal
The soul that stirred our fathers' still aglow;
And should endangered liberty appeal,
The blood of patriots would as freely flow.

. THE END.

www.ingramcontent.com/pod-product-compliance
Lightning Source LLC
Chambersburg PA
CBHW030258170426
43202CB00009B/798